CREATIVE HOMEOWNER® ULTIMATE GUIDE TO

YardandGarden
Sheds

CREATIVE HOMEOWNER®

ULTIMATE GUIDE TO

Yard and Garden
Sheds

PLAN · DESIGN · BUILD

John D. Wagner

CREATIVE HOMEOWNER®, Upper Saddle River, New Jersey

YARD AND GARDEN SHEDS
AUTHORS: John D. Wagner; Saltbox project by Bill Hylton
MANAGING EDITOR: Fran J. Donegan
ASSISTANT EDITOR: Evan Lambert
PHOTO RESEARCHER: Robyn Pollasky
TECHNICAL CONSULTANT: Steve Willson
COPY EDITOR: Marilyn Knowlton
INDEXER: Schroeder Indexing Services
SENIOR DESIGNER: Glee Barre
ILLUSTRATIONS: Ian Worpole, Clarke Barre
FRONT COVER PHOTOGRAPHY: Andrew Klein

CREATIVE HOMEOWNER
VP / PUBLISHER: Brian Toolan
VP / EDITORIAL DIRECTOR: Timothy O. Bakke
PRODUCTION MANAGER: Kimberly H. Vivas,
ART DIRECTOR: David Geer
MANAGING EDITOR: Fran J. Donegan

Printed in China

Current Printing (last digit)
10 9 8 7 6 5 4 3 2 1
Ultimate Guide to Yard and Garden Sheds, First Edition
Library of Congress Control Number: 2005928045
ISBN 10: 1-58011-280-3
ISBN 13: 978-1-58011-280-2

CREATIVE HOMEOWNER®
A Division of Federal Marketing Corp.
24 Park Way, Upper Saddle River, NJ 07458
www.creativehomeowner.com

Metric Equivalents

Length

1 inch	25.4 mm
1 foot	0.3048 m
1 yard	0.9144 m
1 mile	1.61 km

Area

1 square inch	645 mm²
1 square foot	0.0929 m²
1 square yard	0.8361 m²
1 acre	4046.86 m²
1 square mile	2.59 km²

Volume

1 cubic inch	16.3870 cm³
1 cubic foot	0.03 m³
1 cubic yard	0.77 m³

Common Lumber Equivalents

Sizes: Metric cross sections are so close to their U.S. sizes, as noted below, that for most purposes they may be considered equivalents.

Dimensional lumber	1 × 2	19 × 38 mm
	1 × 4	19 × 89 mm
	2 × 2	38 × 38 mm
	2 × 4	38 × 89 mm
	2 × 6	38 × 140 mm
	2 × 8	38 × 184 mm
	2 × 10	38 × 235 mm
	2 × 12	38 × 286 mm
Sheet sizes	4 × 8 ft.	1200 × 2400 mm
	4 × 10 ft.	1200 × 3000 mm
Sheet thicknesses	¼ in.	6 mm
	⅜ in.	9 mm
	½ in.	12 mm
	¾ in.	19 mm
Stud/joist spacing	16 in. o.c.	400 mm o.c.
	24 in. o.c.	600 mm o.c.

Capacity

1 fluid ounce	29.57 mL
1 pint	473.18 mL
1 quart	0.95 L
1 gallon	3.79 L

Weight

1 ounce	28.35g
1 pound	0.45kg

Temperature

Fahrenheit = Celsius × 1.8 + 32
Celsius = Fahrenheit − 32 × ⁵⁄₉

Nail Size & Length

Penny Size	Nail Length
2d	1"
3d	1¼"
4d	1½"
5d	1¾"
6d	2"
7d	2¼"
8d	2½"
9d	2¾"
10d	3"
12d	3¼"
16d	3½"

Safety

Although the methods in this book have been reviewed for safety, it is not possible to overstate the importance of using the safest methods you can. What follows are reminders—some do's and don'ts of work safety—to use along with your common sense.

- Always use caution, care, and good judgment when following the procedures described in this book.

- Always be sure that the electrical setup is safe, that no circuit is overloaded, and that all power tools and outlets are properly grounded. Do not use power tools in wet locations.

- Always read container labels on paints, solvents, and other products; provide ventilation; and observe all other warnings.

- Always read the manufacturer's instructions for using a tool, especially the warnings.

- Use hold-downs and push sticks whenever possible when working on a table saw. Avoid working short pieces if you can.

- Always remove the key from any drill chuck (portable or press) before starting the drill.

- Always pay deliberate attention to how a tool works so that you can avoid being injured.

- Always know the limitations of your tools. Do not try to force them to do what they were not designed to do.

- Always make sure that any adjustment is locked before proceeding. For example, always check the rip fence on a table saw or the bevel adjustment on a portable saw before starting to work.

- Always clamp small pieces to a bench or other work surface when using a power tool.

- Always wear the appropriate rubber gloves or work gloves when handling chemicals, moving or stacking lumber, working with concrete, or doing heavy construction.

- Always wear a disposable face mask when you create dust by sawing or sanding. Use a special filtering respirator when working with toxic substances and solvents.

- Always wear eye protection, especially when using power tools or striking metal on metal or concrete; a chip can fly off, for example, when chiseling concrete.

- Never work while wearing loose clothing, open cuffs, or jewelry; tie back long hair.

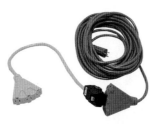

- Always be aware that there is seldom enough time for your body's reflexes to save you from injury from a power tool in a dangerous situation; everything happens too fast. Be alert!

- Always keep your hands away from the business ends of blades, cutters, and bits.

- Always hold a circular saw firmly, usually with both hands.

- Always use a drill with an auxiliary handle to control the torque when using large-size bits.

- Always check your local building codes when planning new construction. The codes are intended to protect public safety and should be observed to the letter.

- Never work with power tools when you are tired or when under the influence of alcohol or drugs.

- Never cut tiny pieces of wood or pipe using a power saw. When you need a small piece, saw it from a securely clamped longer piece.

- Never change a saw blade or a drill or router bit unless the power cord is unplugged. Do not depend on the switch being off. You might accidentally hit it.

- Never work in insufficient lighting.

- Never work with dull tools. Have them sharpened, or learn how to sharpen them yourself.

- Never use a power tool on a workpiece—large or small—that is not firmly supported.

- Never saw a workpiece that spans a large distance between horses without close support on each side of the cut; the piece can bend, closing on and jamming the blade, causing saw kickback.

- When sawing, never support a workpiece from underneath with your leg or other part of your body.

- Never carry sharp or pointed tools, such as utility knives, awls, or chisels, in your pocket. If you want to carry any of these tools, use a special-purpose tool belt that has leather pockets and holders.

CONTENTS

Introduction

Everyone could use a little more storage space, right? If you are like most homeowners, your garage, basement, or crawl space—or maybe all three—are filled to the brim with the lawn mowers, tools, snow-removal equipment, and other gadgets you need to keep your home functioning properly. Some of those items are only used a few times each year; others you may reach for on a regular basis. But no matter how often they are used, they all take up valuable space.

A yard and garden shed offers a chance for you to cut some of that clutter—or at least organize it in a way that makes sense. A shed is an inexpensive storage alternative that is relatively easy to design and build, and it can improve the look and value of your property.

Ultimate Guide to Yard and Garden Sheds provides the inspiration and the how-to instruction to help you add a shed to your yard. The book approaches the shed-acquiring experience from a number of different angles. The first chapter lays out the options open to you—everything from purchasing a shed from a home center or shed retailer to designing and building your own. This chapter opens up the possibilities for you by showing a sample of the shed designs available.

But this book is about building your own shed, and Chapters 2 through 4 lay the groundwork for tackling a shed-building project on your own. These chapters cover basic construction techniques, everything from the tools and materials you will need for the job to framing and roofing. There is even a section on adding electrical power to your shed.

In the second part of the book, you will find guides to building five popular-style sheds. The authors created the designs and then went to work constructing the buildings. Photographers followed the progress of the authors/builders so that you can see how the projects went from empty spaces to ones occupied by attractive, useful outbuildings. Each project includes a list of materials the authors used, a diagram showing how the parts of the sheds go together, and

LEFT This shed is used as a potting shed.

TOP A garden shed is the focal point of this yard.

ABOVE This is the finished gable potting shed that begins on page 144.

dozens of step-by-step photographs that detail the building process. The authors describe what they did and why, and there is a Smart Tip on every right-hand page to help you through your project. Author John Wagner even shares his experiences constructing a shed kit purchased from a shed retailer.

You can use the authors' designs as guides to build your own shed, although you should adjust measurements to suit your needs. Or you can create your own design. Another option is to purchase detailed blueprints for a shed. See page 192 for more information.

Shed Designs. There is a garden shed here for everyone no matter what the storage needs or the skill level of the builder. The Saltbox Shed, page 96, is the largest and most complex project. It measures 12 × 16 feet and features two large doors, a saltbox roof, and cedar siding.

The Gambrel Shed, page 126, has the appearance of a small barn. It can provide ample storage for lawn and garden equipment. You can easily convert the upper area to an additional storage area.

The Gable Shed, page 144, can hold tools or be used as a potting shed. The classic gable roof and cedar shingle siding make it an attractive addition to any yard.

The Attached Shed, page 166, is the easiest to build. This type of structure comes in handy for keeping garden hand tools within easy reach.

The shed kit that begins on page 180 is one of hundreds of designs available. This one features a small porch and ample room inside for storage or enough space to be used as an artist's studio.

TOP RIGHT The gambrel shed begins on page 126.

RIGHT The shed kit begins on page 180.

BELOW Sheds are usually used for storage, but some become relaxing destinations in the yard.

Order Plans to Build Your Own Shed or Outbuilding
To view designs and order plans for a variety of sheds and other types of outbuildings, turn to page 192.

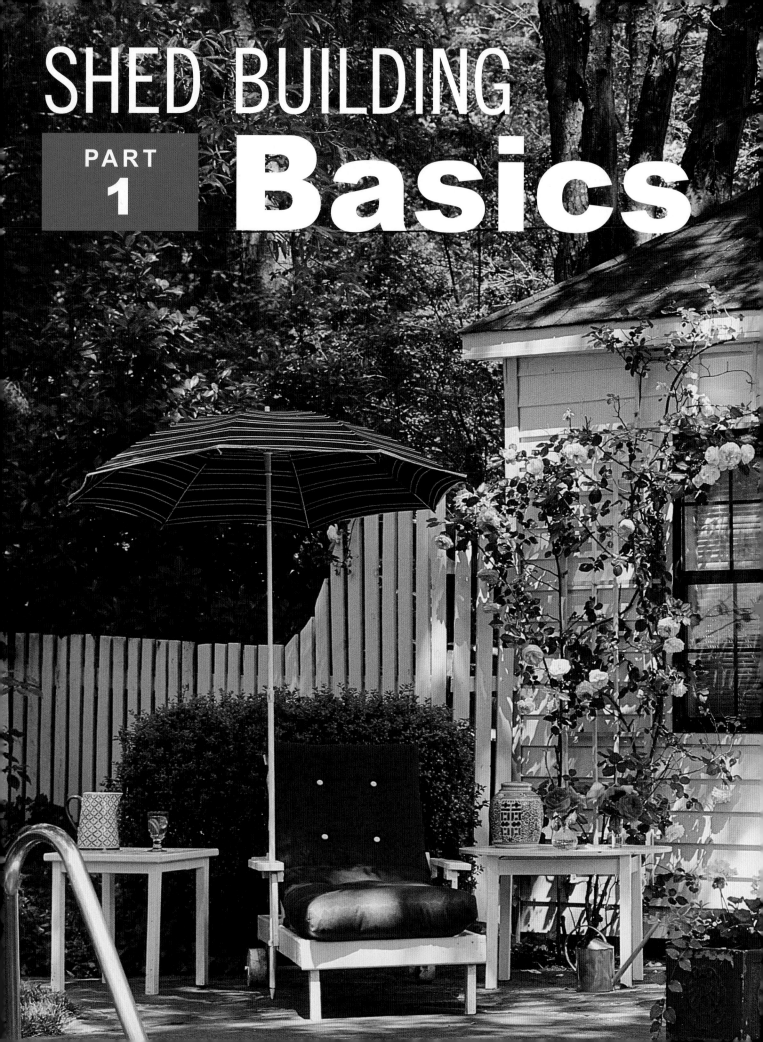

SHED BUILDING

PART 1

Basics

Preparing
to Build

Choosing a Shed Size

The term "shed" has come to include a number of different types of buildings. While most people think of a shed as a place to store tools and equipment, a shed can also be the building in the garden where you transplant plants, a hobby area, a workshop, a playhouse, or even a private place for relaxation. The first step in building a shed is to decide how you will use the building. Determining its intended use will help you pick the right size shed for your needs and for the limitations of your property.

The Right Size. With proper shelving, a shed that is 6 × 8 feet can store your power mover, a trimmer, and a number of hand tools and garden supplies. But you may have to remove some of those items to reach the tool you want. When planning, consider the actual floor space each item will occupy along with enough room to navigate around the building. A rule of thumb is to leave a 12-inch buffer zone around equipment. If the shed will double as a work area, you'll need 36 inches or more between workspaces. For example, allow 8 feet on either end of a table saw.

SHED PLANS

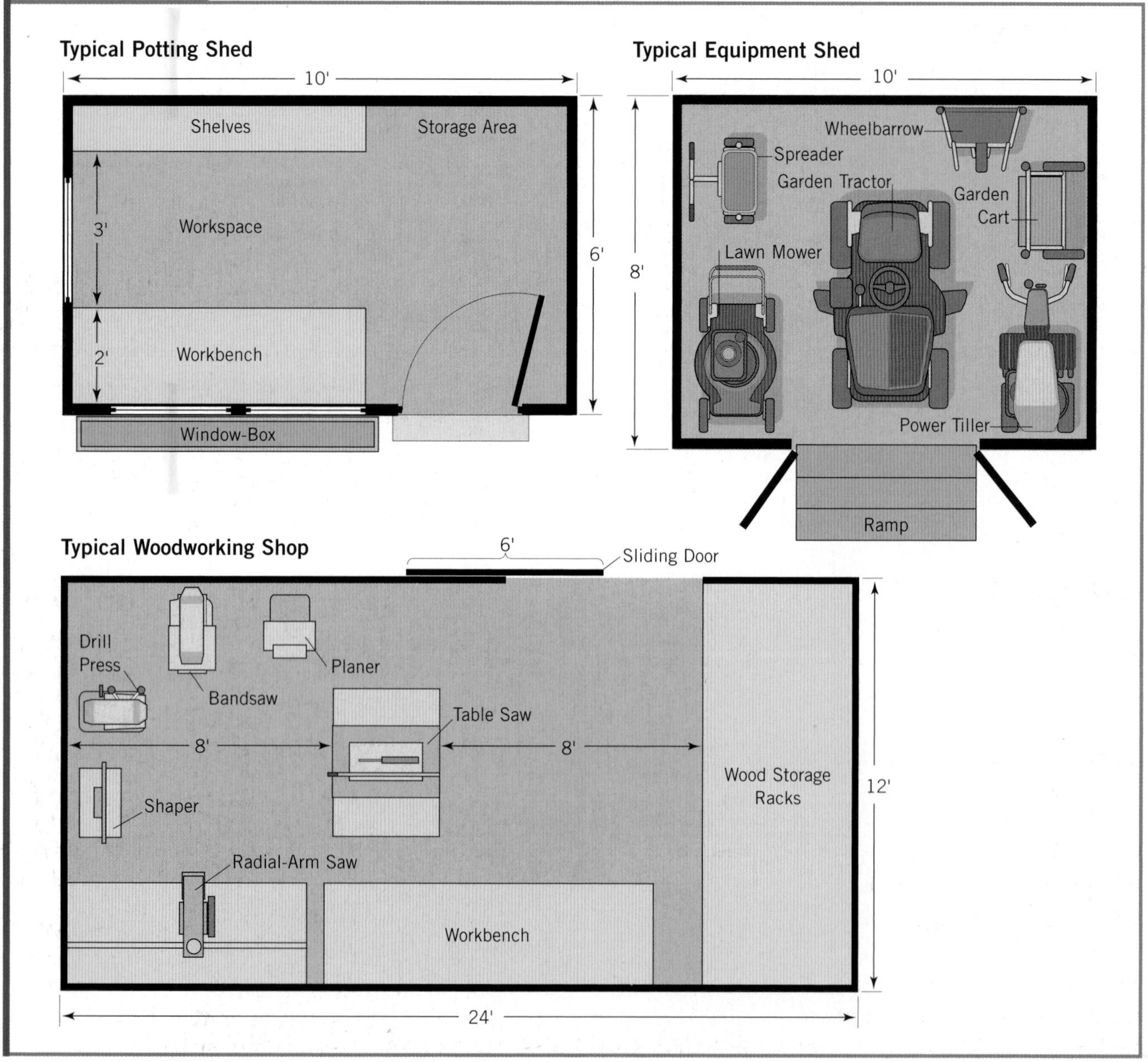

Typical Potting Shed

10'
Shelves	Storage Area
Workspace (3')
Workbench (2')	6'
Window-Box

Typical Equipment Shed

10'
Wheelbarrow
Spreader
Garden Tractor
Garden Cart
Lawn Mower	8'
Power Tiller
Ramp

Typical Woodworking Shop

6' Sliding Door

Drill Press
Bandsaw
Planer
Table Saw
Shaper
8'   8'
Radial-Arm Saw
Wood Storage Racks   12'
Workbench
24'

LEFT AND BELOW
Choose a shed based on how the building will be used. A place to store garden tools need not be as large as a woodshop.

The Right Proportions. The size of the shed should also be in harmony with the other structures on your property. Though a small shed won't draw much attention, a shed that is grossly oversized compared with nearby structures will appear out of place. Scale drawings that compare existing structures with planned buildings give you an indication of relative size. Simple sheds rarely require detailed drawings unless specified by the building department.

SMART TIP 1

When planning for your new shed, set aside some space for things that you will add later. People with tool sheds, potting sheds, and hobby sheds tend to acquire additional tools and materials as time goes on.

Preparing to Build

Picking an Architectural Style

A trip to the local home center or a short session cruising the internet will show you that there are hundreds of shed styles from which to choose. And because the buildings are relatively simple to build, you have the option of trying your hand at designing a shed.

In most cases, the type of roof a shed has and the materials used for roofing and siding will determine the architectural style of the building. "Roof Styles," below, shows the most common rooflines used on garden sheds. Generally speaking, the shed roof type should match the roof types of the surrounding buildings. A gambrel roof will stand out as odd among gables; a shed-style roof can look out of place if it is the only shed-type roof among a group of nearby gambrels.

For roofing material, you have a range of choices. Roofing can be agricultural ribbed metal, asphalt composite shingles, cedar shakes or shingles, or standing-seam metal. Siding choices range even wider, from vertical panels to horizontal cedar shingles or clapboard. Here is where a good sketch can help you visualize your shed.

Try to match the style with the materials. A gambrel shed with vertical plank siding will look remarkably more utilitarian than a saltbox with a cedar shake roof and clapboard siding, which will look quaint and cute by comparison. Mix and match siding and roof types until you find something that pleases you and is in harmony with surrounding structures.

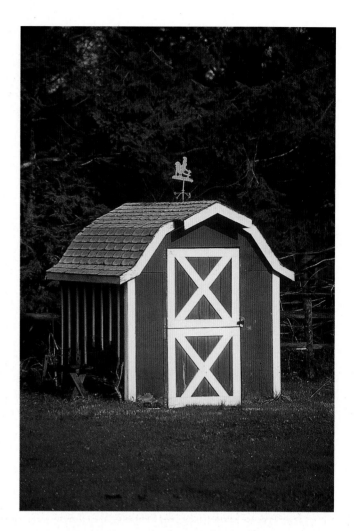

ABOVE House-like features give this garden playhouse an appealing style.

ABOVE RIGHT The gambrel roof and double door make this shed look like a small barn.

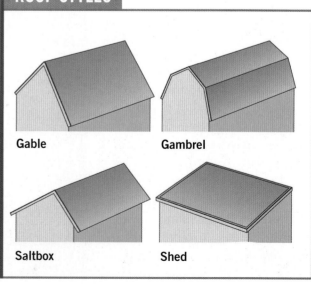

ROOF STYLES

Gable

Gambrel

Saltbox

Shed

LEFT A garden shed
can be hard-working,
or it can be a fun
place for kids to play.

SMART TIP   **1**

You can
embellish any
shed by adding
such items as
window boxes,
weather vanes,
and shutters.

Preparing to Build

Buying a Shed

You can purchase a shed in one of a number of ways. Perhaps the easiest is to go to the local home center and buy one of the products on display. They come in a variety of sizes and styles. Cart it home, and assemble it following the enclosed instructions.

SHED KITS VS. SHED PLANS

Your other options are to purchase a shed kit, build one from plans, or design your own shed. There are a number of good sources of shed kits and plans available. For plans, you'll find that prices are fairly consistent from source to source. But for kits, be sure to compare prices from a number of providers. When you do, you'll find that some shed kit providers are re-marketing kits they have purchased wholesale elsewhere, and their prices vary. Don't be surprised if you find a wide difference in pricing for the exact same kit.

Assembly Required. Standardization is the main advantage of buying a kit. Everything you need is in the box, and the lumber, siding, roofing, and sheet goods are all precut to the exact dimensions needed. Also, professional designers have engineered the structure so that everything fits together right. Items like windows and doors often come preassembled or pre-hung, and decorative or architectural details are already integrated into the structural design.

If that is worth paying a premium, then a kit is for you. But if you're the kind of person who can work from plans, you will save money by creating a design and buying the materials on your own. Or you can purchase a set of plans and build from those.

Understanding Plans. Building plans usually include elevations (renderings of the shed as seen

PLANS

Floor Plan

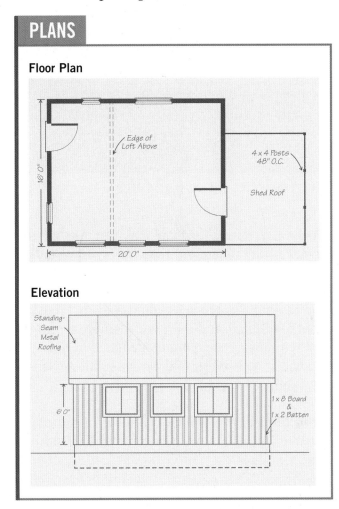

Edge of
Loft Above

4 x 4 Posts
48" O.C.

Shed Roof

16' 0"

20' 0"

Elevation

Standing-
Seam
Metal
Roofing

6' 0"

1 x 8 Board
&
1 x 2 Batten

ABOVE **Provide hooks and shelves to accommodate tools and supplies.**

OPPOSITE **Small sheds place tools in the areas they are needed most.**

SMART TIP   1

Be sure to include shipping charges when comparing prices for kits. The cost to ship a heavy lumber kit can be fairly substantial, ranging up to $1,000.

Preparing to Build

ABOVE Create a design theme to make your shed stand out. A nautical theme fits this small shed used to store pool supplies, accessories, and games.

from each side), framing plans (the lumber skeleton of the shed), and a plan view of the foundation and floor systems. (See "Plans," page 21.) Though someone with even limited experience can probably build a shed without plans, it is better to work from them.

Plans make the work easier by establishing cut lists, lumber lengths, and quantities of items (sheets of plywood, shingles, trim boards, etc.) that you need to acquire to build your shed. They also provide a graphic guide to refer to when assembling the lumber. Even better, they provide you with drawings that help you imagine what the shed will look like when it is completed. Think of how you use plans when assembling a gas grill or knockdown furniture: you may not use all the aspects of the plans, but they help you visualize the finished product in "exploded view" form. If you are like most people, you will figure out the shed assembly as much as you can by first looking at detailed plans and then increasingly abandoning the plans as you gain confidence in how the finished structure should be assembled. Generally, plans are a good guide.

Buying Shed Plans. You can purchase shed plans over the Internet, from any number of books, or from the plans section in the back of this book. Shed plans range in price from $50 to over $300, depending on the size of the building. Some

ABOVE **This shed is used as a greenhouse.**

BELOW **A chair for relaxing and a weathered appearance give this garden structure a down-home feeling.**

shed plan sources will also sell you accessories, like windows, doors, and trim details.

See "Plans for Garden Sheds," page 188.

Another option is to come up with an original design. Most sheds are simple structures that are usually not subject to the same building requirements of houses. If you know how you will use the shed and can estimate its contents, try putting your ideas on paper. Draw on graph paper for the best results.

Think Standard Sizes. You can build any size shed you want, or need, but to make the work go easier, plan in even number dimensions. Dimension lumber, such as 2×4s, 2×6s, and the like, comes in even number length increments starting at 8 feet. Sheet goods, such as plywood and panel siding, come in 4 × 8-foot panels. By building an 8 × 8-foot shed rather than a 7 × 11-foot shed, you will save yourself a great deal of cutting, not to mention saving on the lumber you would ordinarily waste. This is one reason a common shed size is 8 × 12 feet. The proportions create a classic rectangle, and you can use factory lengths of 2-by lumber and standard plywood sheets when framing and sheathing.

SMART TIP   1

For a confidence builder, look for plans or a kit that includes an assembly video or DVD. Watch it all the way through before beginning work.

Preparing to Build

The Right Site

The siting of the shed—where it is positioned on your property—will influence its size. For any location, there must be enough room to accommodate the foundation "footprint" of the shed with a border of clear ground around the perimeter, as the eaves will extend beyond the foundation by 12 to 18 inches. Moreover, the ground must be level, or it must be modified through excavation to be made level. The type of foundation you choose can also level the shed. So your dream location may not be the ideal spot to place your shed,

once you consider the structural and space requirements that will inevitably come into play during the design and building processes.

Setbacks. For most suburban locations, you will likely need to comply with setback requirements. A setback is the minimum allowable distance between the structure you want to build and some other landmark, such as another building, the property line, the street, a wetland, even an easement that is identified only on a deed. Setbacks can range up to 100 feet or more. Adhering to setbacks is no small matter.

Covenants. These are rules set by local communities, neighborhoods, or homeowner associations that can hold sway over aspects of your shed that might surprise you. There may be restrictive covenants that apply to the type of siding or color paint you can use. Check with your homeowner association to see what rules, if any, apply to garden shed construction. In addition to your local building permit authority, a homeowner association's architectural review board may want building plans and elevations (scale sketches of the shed as seen from the side) to review before approval can be granted to build a shed.

Zoning. These requirements may cover shed construction and what you can keep in it. Zoning can regulate everything from roof types—wood shake and shingle roofs are illegal in some fire-prone areas—to live animals. Goats or chickens may seem like a great idea, until you learn that your town bars you from keeping them. You may not even be allowed to have an "outbuilding," as sheds are called. So, early on in the planning stages, check with your town or city's building department for applicable codes and ordinances, and check with your homeowners association for any required architectural review.

Building Codes. In rural locations, building codes, as well as covenants and zoning regulations, may be less restrictive than those found in towns and cities. If you are building a shed on a 5- or 10-acre lot, local building codes and zoning may not impact your design at all. However, it is important to remember that building codes are good guidance for "best-practices" and minimum design standards when building any structure. Your municipality or building code authority—the city or town department that issues the building permit—will tell

Violation of a setback is grounds for dismantling or moving your shed, so call your local building department to determine applicable setbacks for your property.

If your plans don't comply with local zoning laws, you can apply for a variance. Your application will be considered by the local zoning board or the building inspector. Inquire at the building department for zoning variance procedures.

ABOVE Rural areas usually do not have stringent building codes or restrictions on sheds. The structure shown here is a focal point and a destination in a large garden.

SMART TIP 1

Look for shed plans that include construction drawings, which you can submit to your building department when applying for a permit.

Preparing to Build

ABOVE This custom structure is outfitted with all the comforts of home.

you the code to which you must adhere. Increasingly the International Building Code (IBO) is the standard that applies, but some counties, especially in hurricane- or tornado-prone areas, can demand that structures be beefed up beyond IBO requirements.

Building Permits and Inspections. Building permits are usually required for building any structure on your property. If a building permit is required and you don't have one, you may be asked to remove the shed, even long after it is built. However, for small structures you can usually obtain a building permit after the structure is erected and simply pay a fine or extra fee.

The requirements for building permits vary widely. Some towns and cities exempt structures that are built on nonpermanent foundations, such as concrete blocks or wood skids resting on gravel. If you must obtain a building permit, apply for one at your municipality's building department. The type of permit and fee you pay is usually related to the proposed square footage or cost of the shed.

You may need to provide rudimentary building plans and know your square footage. It may take a few days or a week for permit approval, and if you are asking for a zoning variance, your permit may take even longer and be subject to public notice and hearings. Investigate the building permit

ABOVE LEFT Shed kits are available in a variety of shapes.

TOP RIGHT A shed used for garden storage.

MIDDLE A garden shed serves as a spare room.

RIGHT A shed sports decorations.

process early in your planning.

If you require a building permit, your shed will be subject to building inspections. Even though your shed may be a small structure, the building inspector may be called in to approve the foundation, electrical, and framing. You will also be required to get a final inspection once you complete the building. You may also get a "pass with condition," which requests that you make a fix that the inspector doesn't have to reinspect.

SMART TIP   1

Preparing to Build

Be present during the building inspections so that the inspector can tell you what needs to be done to get a "pass." Sometimes you can fix a problem while the inspector is there.

Site Evaluation for Foundations

While most garden sheds do not have stringent construction requirements, they do need to be level. That means altering either the site or the foundation of the shed to make the finished structure level.

The most common way to prepare a non-level site is to excavate dirt out of the area. On steep slopes, you might try building a retaining wall and filling in the low spots with soil. (See "Leveling a Slope," below.)

ABOVE One popular trend is to make playhouses look like miniature versions of full-size homes.

LEVELING A SLOPE

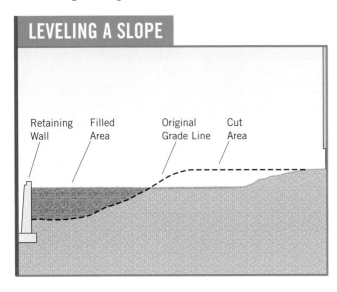

Retaining Wall Filled Area Original Grade Line Cut Area

Note that even a level pad on a steep hill creates a drainage problem, as rainwater will roll down the hill and accumulate behind the shed. So for any steep sloped site, you may have to modify the hill to create a building pad and also install a perimeter drain to pull rainwater away from the foundation.

Soil. If you work in your garden, you may already have an idea of what type of soil you have on your property—whether it's mostly sand, clay, silt, or loam. Soils are rated for their load-bearing capacity—that is, how much weight per square foot they can support without having to be

modified with ¾-inch gravel or even retaining walls. Because sheds are relatively light when compared with a large structure like a house or full-sized barn, it is unlikely that the soil beneath your shed needs to be modified for bearing loads, unless the soil is extremely loamy or heavy with organic matter. In that case, you may have to amend the soil by removing it and replacing it with ¾-inch gravel.

Drainage Requirements. Soil must drain thoroughly, especially in areas where the weather reaches freezing temperatures. Otherwise, moisture retained in the soil will freeze and cause "frost heaving." When wet soil freezes, it can increase in volume by as much as 10 percent, which exerts upward pressure on the soil and your shed's foundation, possibly disrupting the structure. In cold climates, prevent frost-heave damage by installing the base of your foundation below the average frost depth or on well-drained gravel beds. (See Chapter 3, "Foundation Choices," page 52.)

It's also important to have good drainage around your structure for water that runs off of the roof or to accommodate groundwater

OPPOSITE Use your shed as a chance to make a statement in your garden. You can copy the color scheme used on the main house or create something totally different.

SMART TIP

Contact your county extension service for information on soil in your area. Go to www.csrees.usda.gov for a list of offices.

1 Preparing to Build

that may run downhill and be blocked from its normal path by your structure. The soil around your shed should slope away from the foundation, generally at ¼ inch or more per foot for at least 6 feet. If required by heavy water flow on your site, a swale or shallow depression can be used to direct surface water away. A perimeter drain made of perforated pipe can be installed to direct groundwater away from your shed into a drainage ditch if the site is extremely wet and problematic.

Follow the Sun. It's likely you won't be living in your shed, so the orientation (north, south, east, and west) of the shed isn't crucial, but consider how the sun will cast shadows on the shed throughout the seasons. Situating the shed beneath a deciduous tree will give shade in summer and sun in winter, which is ideal for drying the shed out after snow or rain storms. Situating the shed in a shady pine grove may lead to early rotting if there isn't sufficient air circulation and direct sunlight to dry out the wood. And there is the obvious issue of comfort when you're working in the shed. In the summer, the shed can get quite warm. Roof overhangs can shade windows and doors. Windows that face east will collect heat in the morning. West-facing windows will collect heat from the late-afternoon sun.

Frost Depth & Frost Heaving

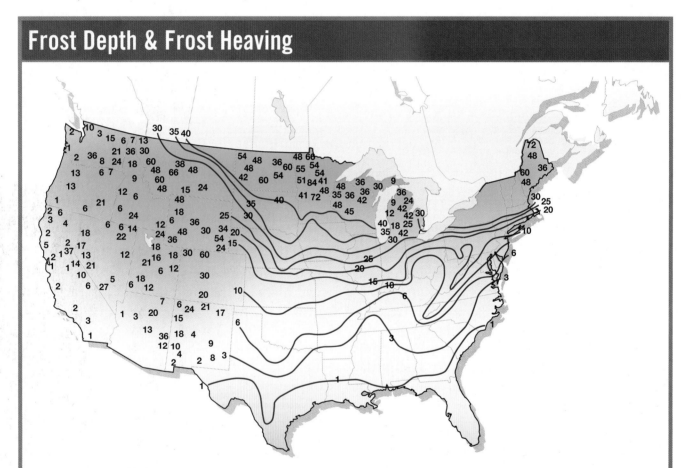

Water expands in volume by about 10 percent when it freezes, which can exert enough pressure to break apart concrete from below. To avoid this problem, called frost heave, piers and footings need to reach below the frost line, which is the average maximum depth of frost penetration. This map shows the average depth of frost throughout the U.S. In the western and northern parts of the country, as well as in Canada, freezing patterns vary so much that zoning is all but impossible. Even within zones, frost depths can vary depending on local weather patterns, altitude, and soil. Local building codes strictly regulate foundation depth and construction. To be safe, you should always consult the local building inspector before starting a foundation project.

SMART TIP 1

To cool the
interior of your
shed naturally,
choose a design
with large eaves.
Long eaves block
sunlight during
the warm-
weather months.

Preparing to Build

Shed Ideas

OPPOSITE Sheds don't need to be placed on the ground. This elevated structure looks like a tree house.

LEFT Be sure to include shelving and other storage to meet your needs. Don't forget about electrical and water if needed.

BELOW You will see the shed from the house and other parts of the yard—so make it attractive.

2

Tools and
Materials

Tools

Good tools can help you do a good job of building your shed or any type of building or outbuilding. You don't need to invest in top-of-the-line tools, but good-quality mid-priced tools will go a long way in helping you work efficiently and safely. This chapter discusses the basic tools you will need for this type of construction project, including tools for layout, cutting, attachment, and working safely. You will also learn how to select the right materials, including distinguishing from among the different types of lumber available.

CONSTRUCTION LEVELS

It is essential to build any structure plumb, level, and square. To do that, you will at least want to have a 4-foot spirit level for checking framing, and a line level and mason's string for checking long spans.

Spirit Levels. Spirit levels come in many lengths. A 4-foot model is best for working with framing. You can also extend its useful range by resting it on a long straight 2×4.

Digital Levels. Unlike spirit levels, digital levels beep when they are level or plumb. The tools never go out of whack because you can reset them electronically. Some electronic levels also work as inclinometers to give you the angle of rafters. That feature can be handy when you have to match roof pitches in separate, distant locations.

Water Level. A water level is basically colored water in a long clear tube with gradation marks on both ends. Because water seeks its own level no matter what the distance or terrain, you can use the tool for long-distance level checks. Once any air bubbles are removed, stretch the hose from one place to another (even up and down over rough terrain) and the water line at both ends will be level.

Safety Tools

Common sense should tell you not to do construction work without first having some basic safety equipment, such as eye and ear protection. Wear goggles or safety glasses that have aerated side guards whenever you work with power tools. The U.S. Occupational Safety and Health Administration (OSHA) recommends that hearing protection be worn when the noise level exceeds 85 decibels (dB) for an eight-hour workday. When you consider that a circular saw emits 110 dB, however, it is clear that even much shorter exposure to loud noises can contribute to hearing impairment. Both insert and muff-type ear protectors are available; whichever you choose, be sure it has a noise reduction rating (NRR) of a least 20 dB.

If you're sensitive to dust, and whenever you cut pressure-treated wood, it's a good idea to wear a dust mask. Two basic kinds of respiratory protection are available: disposable dust masks and cartridge-type respirators. A dust mask will allow you to avoid inhaling dust and fine particles. Respirators have a replaceable filter. Both are available for protection against nontoxic and toxic dust and mist. Whichever you buy, look for a stamp indicating that the National Institute for Occupational Safety and Health/Mine Safety and Health Administration (NIOSH/MSHA) has approved it for your specific job. When you can taste or smell the contaminant or when the

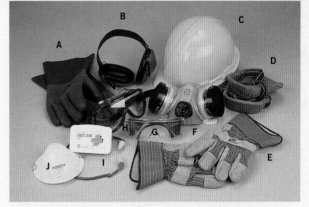

Safety equipment to have on hand includes rubber gloves (A), ear protectors (B), hard hat (C), kneepads (D), work gloves (E), respirator (F), safety glasses (G), safety goggles (H), ear plugs (I), particle mask (J).

mask starts to interfere with normal breathing, it's time for a replacement.

Work gloves are also advisable when you're moving wood or doing other rough jobs. Similarly, heavy-duty work boots will protect your feet. Steel toes will prevent injuries to your toes from dropped boards or tools, and flexible steel soles will protect your feet from a puncture by a stray nail.

Spirit levels are indispensable tools for carpentry. A 4-ft. level is needed for many aspects of framing and finishing; smaller levels are good for doors and windows.

Digital levels are used much like spirit levels, but they have a digital readout. Most kinds will also emit a beep when they are held at level or plumb.

For grading sloped land and laying out level foundations, you'll need to use a transit, a builder's level, or a laser level. These tools allow you to sight a level line across large distances. These are expensive items, so you should rent them, if possible, when you're building from scratch.

MASONRY TOOLS

Whether you're working with concrete, brick, or unit masonry (such as concrete block), you'll need many of the same basic masonry tools. You can

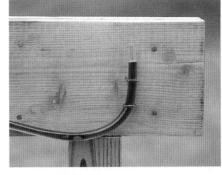

A water level is used for marking level points across long distances. They are especially useful for checking formwork before pouring a foundation.

easily rent many expensive items, so check before you buy a tool that you may not use often. You'll need trowels and floats for the placing and finishing of concrete, and a bull float (made of magnesium or steel) or a darby (made of wood) to finish the upper layer of curing concrete. With a finishing trowel, you can create a smooth surface once the concrete is leveled; then you'll use edging and jointing trowels on the surface of the smooth concrete. An edging trowel makes a rounded edge on a concrete slab, which is safer and more durable than a sharp edge. A groover has a ridge down the center of its blade to form grooves or control joints. Jointers are metal rods (round or square) attached to a handle that you use to create various mortar joints when working with brick and concrete block.

Masonry tools: rubber float (A), striking tool (B), mason's trowel (C), wood float (D), 5-lb. hammer (E), magnesium float (F), jointer (G), brickset (H), notched trowel (I), and groover (J).

An air-powered nail gun has a clip of banded nails that feed into the gun and are fired with a trigger squeeze. While handy, it is not cost-effective for small projects.

DRIVING NAILS & SCREWS

Hammers Pros often use a 20- to 24-ounce waffle-head, or serrated, straight-claw framing hammer. Wooden (hickory) handles tend to absorb vibration better than fiberglass handles, so some people think wooden handles lessen your chances of developing repetitive motion ailments like carpal tunnel syndrome. If you're not used to manual labor, a 24-ounce hammer may be too heavy for you and you'll probably be better off with the 20- or 16-ounce size.

Nail Gun. A pneumatic, or air-driven, nail gun, which uses a magazine that holds up to 100 or more nails, can take much of the tedium out of repetitive nailing. But you pay a price: nail guns are expensive and heavy, and you need compressors and hoses to run them. Nail guns really don't pay for themselves—purchased or rented—unless you have a great amount of nailing to do all at one time.

Most guns handle 6d through 16d nails. You'll need a compressor, gasoline or electric, and at least 100 feet of air hose. If you have a choice, go with the quieter electric compressor. Also, make sure you set the compressor's in-line regulator to the pressure required for the tool you'll be using.

Power Drill. A corded or battery-powered drill is essential not only for driving wood screws but

This basic collection includes a standard twist drill bit (A), spade bit (B), masonry bit (C), hole saw (D), single-twist auger bit (E), Forstner bit (F), and adjustable screw pilot bit (G).

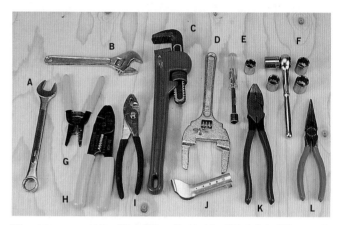

Wrenches: combination (A), adjustable (B), pipe (C), spud (D), nut driver (E), socket (F); pliers: electrician's (G), multipurpose tool (H), slip-joint (I), cable stripper (J), cutting (K), and needle-nose (L).

A socket wrench kit or a set of combination wrenches is necessary for driving nuts onto bolts. For some jobs, you will need extra-deep sockets and an extended handle.

Woodworking tools: tool belt (A), belt sander (B), smooth plane (C), scraper (D), long reel-type tape (E), screwdrivers (F), utility knife (G), measuring tape (H), sandpaper (I), wood chisels (J), wood files (K), and a pry bar (L).

also for quickly and precisely drilling holes. If cost is an issue, buy a plug-in heavy-duty ⅜-inch drill with variable speeds. If you can afford the extra cost, you'll find a cordless drill even handier. Cordless drills come in an array of voltage ratings; the higher the voltage, the more powerful the drill. A 12-volt drill generally is powerful enough to fill all your needs.

OTHER BASIC TOOLS

Drill Bits. The standard twist drill bit bores holes in wood, plastic, or metal. Spade bits quickly make large holes in wood, but not as cleanly as other bits. Masonry bits drill holes into brick and concrete. Hole saws make large, accurate holes up to several inches in diameter. Single-twist auger bits have a small cone-shaped point at the tip to make them more accurate than traditional bits. Forstner bits cut holes with very little tearout. An adjustable screw pilot bit will stop at a predetermined depth and cut a countersink all in one step.

Wrenches and Pliers. Combination wrenches, adjustable wrenches, nut drivers, and socket wrenches have countless applications. You'll use pipe and spud wrenches when working with plumbing. For wiring, electrician's pliers, the multipurpose tool, and the cable ripper come in handy. Slip joint, diagonal-cutting, and needlenose pliers have many practical uses.

Woodworking Tools. Use a tool belt when carrying nails and screws. Sanders, planes, and files help even out surfaces. Use measuring tapes to lay out the site and measure for cuts. Use knives and chisels to cut small amounts of material in places where a saw is not practical. You can use a pry bar as a lever in a variety of building situations. A screwdriver is often the only practical means of driving a screw.

SQUARES

For accurate layout, you'll need a framing square. It's etched for layout of plumb and seat cuts for common rafters or hip rafters, plus degrees of angle for use as a protractor. A speed square—a heavy-duty aluminum right triangle—

is great for guiding your saw and marking lumber, and also is etched with information. A combination square and a sliding T-bevel are helpful in marking cut lines on framing.

Framing Square. A framing square is an L-shaped tool made of steel or aluminum. It is indispensable

A framing square is a useful tool for checking stud layout, squaring up corners, and marking long cuts. For roof framing, a framing square with rafter tables is a useful addition to your tool kit.

when cutting rafters, marking cut lines on lumber, and making sure corners are square. Like the speed square, the framing square has figures etched into it. The figures sometimes include extensive rafter tables.

Combination Square. A combination square is a ruler with a sliding bracket mounted to it at 90 degrees. The bracket has a second surface, which you can use to make 45-degree cut lines on lumber. Some squares have a pointed metal scribe to mark work for cutting. This tool is handy, but the speed square will serve most of your needs.

A combination square has a sliding blade, for making short measurements, checking right angles, and marking lumber cuts. Some have a spirit level.

SMART TIP

Cordless tools are great for shed building, especially if you are working away from an electrical receptacle. Buy an extra battery so that your tool will be ready whenever you are.

Using Saws Safely

Set up a safe cutting station on heavy-duty boards or thick plywood fastened to sturdy sawhorses on level ground. When you cut large pieces, you must have something to support the wood that's hanging in midair; otherwise it will droop and bind your cut, increasing the risk of kickback.

Kickback happens when a blade binds in the cut or the teeth try to take too much of a bite, and the saw jumps back at you. It happens quickly and is quite dangerous. You can buy antikickback blades, which have modified tooth designs, but you can best reduce kickback by not rushing a cut and by stabilizing your work. Always stay away from directly behind the saw, and don't remove the saw from the workpiece until the blade has stopped.

When cutting wood where you'll install it, support the wood, preferably on sawhorses. Keep your hands as far as possible from the cut, and clearly sight your cut line to make sure it's free of obstructions such as nails or extension cords. Firmly place wood on a cutting surface; never cut wood held in your hand.

Sliding T-bevel. Often called a bevel square or bevel gauge, this tool is useful for some complicated framing problems. You can set a sliding T-bevel at any angle and use it to transfer the same angle from one place to another.

SAWS

Though framing doesn't demand the precise cuts that finish carpentry does, you still need high-quality saws with sharp blades. With power saws, a 7¼-inch circular saw is a practical choice. Look for one with good balance that is light enough for you to maneuver and easy to adjust for angle and depth. Make sure it has a comfortable handle. A table saw also adds tremendous capability to a project because you can rip sheets of plywood and boards quickly and accurately.

Handsaws. Crosscut saws are versatile handsaws about 24 inches long, with seven or eight teeth per inch. You can also buy specialized trim saws and rip saws. Backsaws—shorter, stiffer and broader than crosscut saws, with finer teeth—are good for detail and trimwork. Hacksaws are essential for cutting pipe, nails, and other materials too tough for a wood saw. Keyhole saws have a narrow-

You'll need a variety of handsaws for framing and finish work: crosscut saws are useful for making cuts where it's impractical to maneuver a circular saw.

A 7¼-in. mid-priced circular saw is the best model for most do-it-yourselfers. Battery-powered models are available for sites located far from a source of electricity.

point blade handy for making small cutouts; stubbier versions with coarser teeth are called utility saws and are good for cutting outlet and other openings in drywall. Coping saws are used mainly to join curved-profile moldings.

Circular Saw. A circular saw is capable of quickly crosscutting, ripping, and beveling boards or sheets of plywood. The most popular saws are those that take a 7¼-inch blade. With this blade size you can cut to a maximum depth of about 2½ inches at 90 degrees. Some contractors use circular saws with larger blades for cutting posts in one pass, but a 7¼-inch circular saw is easier to control, and it allows you to cut anything as large as a 6×6 with a second pass. Smaller saws are also available, some of which are battery powered. These saws are often referred to as trim saws. Battery-driven models can be useful in situations when extension cords would get in the way.

Don't judge power saw performance by horsepower rating alone. Also look at the amperage that the motor draws. Low-cost saws may have 9- or 10-amp motors with drive shafts and arbors running on rollers or sleeve bearings. A contractor-grade saw generally is rated at 12 or 13 amps and is made with more-durable ball bearings. Plastic housings are no longer the mark of an inferior tool; however, a flimsy base plate made of stamped metal is. A thin base won't stay as flat as an extruded or cast base. To minimize any chance of electric shock, be sure that your saw is double insulated. Most saws have a safety switch that you must depress before the trigger will work.

Reciprocating Saw. This saw comes in handy for cutting rough openings in sheathing, fixing framing errors, cutting nail-embedded wood, or cutting the last ½ inch that your circular saw can't get to when you cut to a perpendicular line. Buy plenty of wood- and metal-cutting blades, but don't confuse the two. Wood blades have larger, more-offset teeth than the small-toothed metal-cutting blades.

Power Miter Saw. For angle cuts, you'll want to use a power miter saw, also called a chop saw. This tool is simply a circular saw mounted on a pivot assembly, which enables you to make precise

A reciprocating saw, used for making rough cuts, is good for demolition work. It's also handy for cutting openings for a window, door, or roof vent.

straight and angled crosscuts in boards. You can buy chop saws that handle 10- to 15-inch blades. A 12-inch saw is often the best value for the money. Use a 60-tooth combination-cut carbide blade for all around work.

Ladders, Scaffolds & Fall Protection

Most accidents in the construction industry are a result of falling. The risks increase as you move higher on a building. However, you can work safely by using the ladders, scaffolds, and fall-arrest devices on the market today. When you use these systems properly, you can protect yourself and anyone else working on your project, and increase overall job productivity.

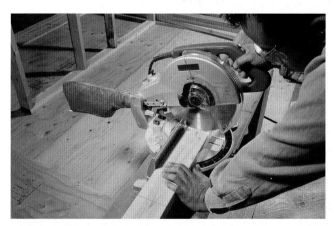

A power miter saw may be the right choice to speed up your production if you don't have enough room for a table or radial-arm saw in the work area.

LADDERS

There are three basic kinds of ladders: stepladders, fold-up (articulated) ladders, and extension ladders. Stepladders are stable on a level surface, but you should never use one on a slope. The hazard with a stepladder is that the higher you go, the more unstable the ladder is. If you find you're working with your feet on or near the top three steps, you should move to a scaffold work platform or extension ladder.

Fold-up ladders are great for working mid-distances between 4 and 12 feet off the ground. These ladders are handy because you can extend the ladder and lock it straight to act as a standard, one-section ladder, lock it in an A position to act as a stepladder, or fold it into an M shape or into an upside-down U shape as a mini-scaffold on which you can place certified scaffold planks.

Extension ladders are used mostly for high outdoor work. Depending on the performance rating you use, these ladders will support the weight of a worker plus material (shingles, lumber, one end of a beam). Extension ladders are available in a wide range of sizes, typically from 20 to 50 feet.

You'll find each kind of ladder in metal (usually aluminum) or fiberglass, and many stepladders and extension ladders made of wood. The type you'll choose depends on the work at hand and how much you want to spend.

Ratings. Ladders are rated for the weight they can hold. You'll see a sticker on most ladders identifying their type. Type III ladders are light-duty and can carry 200 pounds per rung or step. Type II are medium-duty and can carry 225 pounds per rung or step. Type I ladders are heavy-duty industrial ladders and can hold 250 pounds per rung. Type IA ladders are extra heavy-duty and can hold 300 pounds per rung. Type I ladders are well worth the extra money for their greater safety margin.

Safe Use. When you use a straight ladder, set it against a vertical surface at the proper angle. As a rule of thumb, the distance between the base of the ladder and the structure should be one-quarter the ladder's extension. If your ladder extends 16 feet, for example, it should be about 4 feet from the wall. Anything steeper increases the risk that the ladder will topple backward when someone is on it, especially near the top. Anything shallower risks that the ladder may kick out or slide. Bear in mind these two rules for safety: allow the top of the ladder to extend about 3 feet past your work area; and if you're working near electrical lines use a fiberglass ladder.

Lumber

Wood is one of the most important materials you'll buy for your project, so you should purchase the best quality you can afford.

HARDWOOD & SOFTWOOD

Wood is generally divided into two broad categories: hardwood and softwood. Common hardwoods include ash, birch, cherry, poplar, black walnut, maple, northern red oak, and white oak. Hardwoods come from slow-growing deciduous trees (trees that lose their leaves in winter); they are expensive and generally quite strong. Many hardwoods have beautiful grain patterns and are well suited to woodworking.

LADDERS

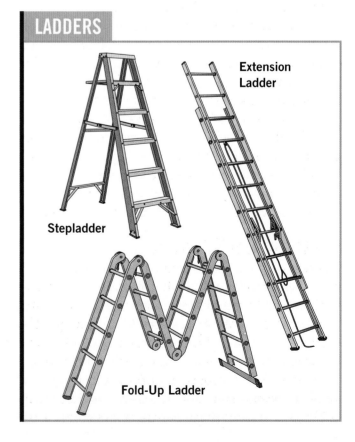

Extension Ladder

Stepladder

Fold-Up Ladder

But they are only used in the most expensive timber-frame construction.

Softwoods come from fast-growing, cone-bearing trees called conifers, or evergreens. Usually much less expensive than hardwoods and widely available at lumberyards, softwoods account for nearly all the lumber used in framing and construction. Though hardwoods are normally stronger because they're more dense, softwoods are certainly more than strong enough for utility framing.

Douglas fir, hemlock, eastern white pine, southern yellow pine, and spruce are all softwoods commonly used for framing. Douglas fir is used for most rough construction, especially along the Pacific Coast, where it is milled. In the South and East you're more likely to find southern pine. There are two other softwoods you might see, redwood and western red cedar, which aren't normally used for framing because of their expense. These species are excellent for exterior siding, trim, and decks because of their exceptional durability and natural resistance to decay.

Sawmills cut softwoods into standard dimensions and lengths. That's why the lumber is sometimes called dimension lumber. Unlike ordering hardwood, ordering softwood framing lumber generally doesn't require that you ask for a specific species of wood. You simply order by dimension and grade. The lumberyard has already made a softwood choice for you by buying whatever wood is available for your region. The lumber is often simply stamped SPF for spruce, pine, fir; it can be any one of these softwood species. To understand lumber and how to use it properly, you need to know about the properties of a tree and the milling process.

SAPWOOD & HEARTWOOD

There are two kinds of wood in all trees: sapwood and heartwood. Sapwood, as its name implies, carries sap to the leaves. The heartwood is the dense center of the tree. Trees that grow quickly (softwoods) tend to have disproportionately more sapwood. In fact, young trees consist of almost all sapwood. This is important to know when you buy lumber because sapwood and heartwood function differently in buildings. Heartwood, for instance,

is used in exposed conditions or for special structural members because it is stronger and more durable. Sapwood is better suited for use as planks, siding, wall studs, and most other building components. And unless it's treated, sapwood lumber is more susceptible to decay than heartwood lumber.

MILLED DIMENSIONS

A piece of lumber has two sizes: nominal and actual. A 2×4 may start out at 2×4 inches (its nominal size) when it comes off a log, but it soon shrinks when it is dried. Then it shrinks again when it is planed. A 2×4 soon becomes 1½ × 3½ inches—the lumber's actual size. For wood lengths, the nominal and actual lengths are almost always the same. When you buy a 10-foot 2×4, it is usually 10 feet long (plus an inch or two).

Some lumberyards charge for lumber by the board foot, though increasingly yards are charging by the individual stick, or piece of lumber. If your lumberyard charges you by the board foot, here's how to figure it: take the

LUMBER GRADES AND CUTS

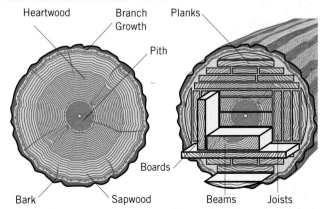

Two types of wood grow within all trees: sapwood and heartwood. Studs are typically sawed from the sapwood area, large-dimension and higher-grade boards and planks from the inner areas, and beams from the heartwood area.

nominal thickness, multiply it by the nominal width and the length, and divide by 12. A 10-foot 2×6 (usually written 2×6×10' in the industry) would be 10 board feet.

GRADES

Besides sapwood and heartwood distinctions, many other wood features come into play, including moisture content, strength, number of knots, and appearance. A standardized system of grading rates wood for many of these qualities. The lower the grade, the poorer the quality.

Lumber grading for structural-grade lumber is complex, with categories, grades, and subgrades. For most framing, you'll find four lumber categories: select structural, No. 1, No. 2, and No. 3. The higher the number, the weaker the wood; the weaker the wood, the less distance you can span. A 2×8 hemlock-fir marked select-structural used as a joist and framed 16 inches on center might span 14 feet 2 inches, for instance, but a No. 3 grade only 11 feet. The wood gets weaker because there are more knots and less consistent grain as you move away from the select-structural grade. You also pay more for stronger wood. For structural framing—joists, rafters, ridge boards—the typical lumber grade is No. 2.

When evaluating 2×4s, you'll find that there are three other names for the No. 1, No. 2, and No. 3 categories. Construction grade corresponds to No. 1; Standard-Better to No. 2; and Utility to

No. 3. (A final category, Economy, is for non-structural use.) For wall framing, use No. 2 (Standard or Better) for load-bearing and most other walls. Many yards don't stock weaker No. 3 (Utility). Because it's hard to sort this all out, and using utility lumber yields only marginal savings, you can safely buy No. 2 lumber and use it for your entire project.

All lumber has a high moisture content when it is milled. So it is either air-dried or kiln-dried for construction use. The acceptable maximum moisture content for framing wood at a lumberyard is 19 percent. Often the grade stamp for construction lumber will say "KD-19" (kiln-dried 19 percent).

ROUGH-SAWN NATIVE GREEN LUMBER

Available from some local sawmills, native green lumber's moisture content is usually high because it's sold unseasoned. Also, it's not cut as precisely as standard lumber. A 2×8 can be 2¼ × 8½ inches, for instance, or 2 × 7¼ inches. It's unpredictable. Additionally, native green lumber is not as structurally stable as kiln-dried or air-dried dimension lumber. The wood is heavy and hard to work with, and it cracks and splits as it dries. Native green lumber is inexpensive, however, and it is often used to frame rough structures such as sheds or barns. Also, you can nail it in place soaking wet when you use it for board-and-batten siding.

PRESSURE-TREATED LUMBER

Pressure-treated (PT) wood is lumber that's been soaked under pressure with an insecticide and a fungicide, which ward off pests and decay, respectively. It's intended for use anywhere the wood contacts the ground (decks and piers), experiences sustained moisture levels (sills, outdoor stairs), or is subject to insect infestation (any exposed part of your structure in termite areas). PT lumber is mostly southern yellow pine, although some other pines, firs, and hemlocks are used occasionally.

In the past, the most common kind of PT wood was treated with chromated copper arsenate (CCA), a compound that chemically bonds with the wood. CCA-treated lumber has a green

Nominal & Actual Lumber Sizes

Nominal Size (in.)	Actual Size (in.)	Nominal Size (in.)	Actual Size (in.)
1x2	¾ x 1½	2x2	1½ x 1½
1x4	¾ x 3½	2x4	1½ x 3½
1x6	¾ x 5½	2x6	1½ x 5½
1x8	¾ x 7½	2x8	1½ x 7½
1x10	¾ x 9¼	2x10	1½ x 9½
1x12	¾ x 11¼	2x12	1½ x 11¼
⁵⁄₄x2	1 x 1½	4x4	3½ x 3½
⁵⁄₄x4	1 x 3½	6x6	5½ x 5½

Rough-sawn green lumber can be ordered from some lumberyards and sawmills. It is beefier (a 2x4 being much closer to 2 in. thick), rougher, and more irregular than finished lumber.

tint from the oxidation of the copper. The retention level achieved during treatment determined its use.

CCA (and to some extent, all chemical treatments) is controversial: some studies have shown that the arsenic in it dissolves back into the environment under certain circumstances. Manufacturers of these products have voluntarily withdrawn most CCA-treated lumber from the residential market. To fill the void, manufacturers have replaced CCA products with those treated with non-arsenic copper compounds.

Most companies have proprietary formulas and market the products under different brand names.

Cautions. Check product data sheets for proper uses of the new treated lumber. One difference you will notice right away is that the signature green tint of CCA-treated lumber is replaced by a brown color that eventually weathers to a gray color as the wood is exposed to the elements.

The other major difference is that there is some evidence that the chemicals used to treat lumber are more corrosive than CCA. This could be a problem with some types of fasteners. Again, check with the manufacturer about fastener selection. Some studies have shown that stainless-steel fasteners offer the best resistance to corrosion. A second choice may be nails and screws finished with a polymer coating.

Grade Stamps

A typical grade stamp identifies the mill, the grading service's name, the moisture content, the grade, and the species.

The mill identification number isn't really important. The same with the grading service. The species mark is mostly a curiosity, too. But look closely at the biggest word in the grading stamp. You should see a word like STAND, which stands for Standard, the grade you'll use for standard residential-grade light framing. Next, look at the moisture designation. Here's where you'll see KD for kiln-dried, S-DRY, MC, or S-GRN. These are the moisture content ratings mentioned in the "Grades," page 44.

But no matter how much you know, the lumberyard will have already made most framing lumber choices for you, at least in terms of species. You'll simply specify the grade. Check the grading stamp at the yard to make sure you've picked up the right kind of wood.

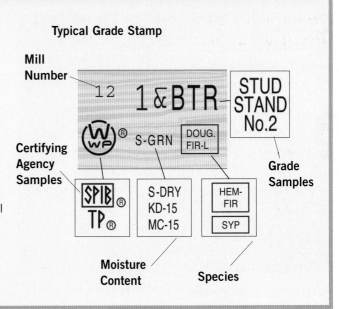

Typical Grade Stamp

Common Lumber Problems

As with any organic material that gains and loses water, wood swells when it is moist and shrinks as it dries. This can lead to warping (uneven shrinking during drying), checking (cracks along growth rings), bowing (end-to-end deviation from the plane of the board's wide face), twisting (spiral or torsional distortion), and cupping (deviation from a flat plane, edge to edge). Softwoods like pine, Douglas fir, and cedar are particularly vulnerable.

Given the demand on the nation's forests for wood, many lumber companies have shortened their harvesting cycles or have planted fast-growing trees. When these trees are harvested, they yield juvenile wood, which can give you problems. Juvenile wood encompasses the first 5 to 20 annual growth rings of any tree, and when it's used for lumber, it doesn't have the same strength as mature wood. You may get bouncy floors, buckled walls, weakened joints, and poorly fitting windows and doors. Even kiln-dried juvenile wood can warp because of nonuniform growth-ring distribution. Inspect the lumber you're buying, and look for telltale signs of juvenile wood, such as uneven grain distribution and warping, and refuse wood that is not up to par.

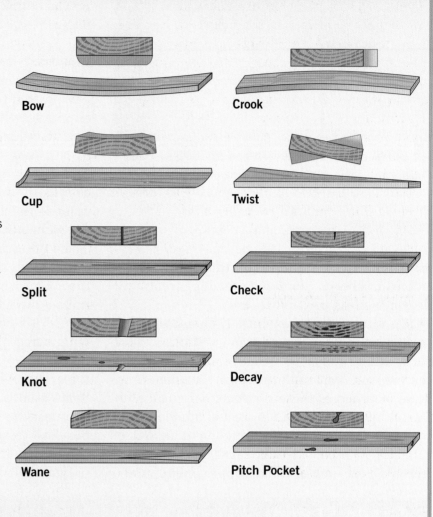

Bow

Crook

Cup

Twist

Split

Check

Knot

Decay

Wane

Pitch Pocket

Rot-resistant pressure-treated lumber is commonly used on foundation sills.

Plywood & Panel Products

Depending on your design, you might need plywood for floor decking and wall and roof sheathing. Plywood comprises an odd number of thin veneer layers of wood, called plies. The veneers are cross-laminated so the grain of one ply runs perpendicular to another. The veneers are glued and sandwiched together and then heated to over 300°F under 200 pounds per square inch (psi) of pressure. Standard plywood thicknesses are $\frac{5}{16}$, $\frac{3}{8}$, $\frac{7}{16}$, $\frac{15}{32}$, $\frac{1}{2}$, $\frac{5}{8}$, $\frac{23}{32}$, $\frac{3}{4}$, and $1\frac{1}{8}$ inches. If you order $\frac{1}{2}$- and $\frac{3}{4}$-inch plywood for your job, you'll most likely get $\frac{15}{32}$- and $\frac{23}{32}$-inch plywood, respectively. Panels are almost always 4×8 feet after factory trimming. Corner to corner, panels sometimes can be slightly out of square, but not enough to cause problems.

Every piece of plywood has a face veneer and a back veneer. These are the outside plies. The plies under the face and back veneers are called crossbands, and the center ply is called the core. The core can be either veneer or solid lumber. Some plywoods even have fiberglass or particleboard at their cores. Veneer-core plywood is stronger than lumber-core plywood, but lumber-core plywood can hold screws better at its edges.

Used in the right applications, plywood is strong and adds stiffness to walls and strength to floors. Besides conventional sheathing plywood, you can buy treated, fire-retardant, and waterproof plywood for special applications.

OTHER PANEL PRODUCTS

Panel products other than plywood, called nonveneer or reconstituted wood-product panels, are sometimes used for sheathing. (Check this with your local building department.) Some of these panels are just as strong—and cheaper—than plywood. The products are called reconstituted because they're made from wood particles or wood strands that are bonded together with adhesive into 4×8-foot sheets.

Structural Particleboard. Also called flakeboard or chipboard, particleboard is simply a panel of wood particles held together by hot-pressed resin. Some exterior-rated products have a layer of resin or wax on the outside to repel water. The glue used in these products is urea formaldehyde or phenol-formaldehyde adhesive. Some building-code organizations allow you to use structural particleboard as an underlayment or a subfloor. Be sure to check with your code officials.

Oriented-Strand Board. Usually called OSB, this product also uses strands of wood, but the layers are crossed so that the direction of the grain of each layer is at 90 degrees to the previous layer, just as plywood is cross-laminated to give it strength. The three to five layers of strands in OSB are bonded together with phenolic resin. These panels have a smooth face and are often rated for structural applications. Waferboard, sometimes called strand board, is a similar product, but without the alternating layers of OSB.

Composite Board. Basically a hybrid of plywood and particleboard, composite board has a reconstituted-wood-particle center but a face and back of plywood veneer.

SMART TIP

Plywood comes in 4 x 8-foot sheets, but many home centers sell 2 x 4-foot sheets as well. The smaller panels are more expensive per square foot, but they can be handy in a pinch.

Common Wood Panel Products

Plywood consists of several thin layers glued together with their grains running in alternating directions. Plywood comes in several thicknesses, grades, and ratings that indicate their use.

Structural particleboard is made from wood chips and sawdust glued together typically with urea formaldehyde resin into 4 x 8-ft. sheets. Its uses are often restricted by local building codes.

Oriented-strand board (OSB) is made from opposingly placed strips of scrap wood held together by adhesives. Some codes allow it for use as sheathing and subflooring.

Engineered Framing Products

Some engineered wood products were created in response to declining wood quality and rising costs. High-quality long beams of Douglas fir are expensive and few lumberyards will stock them. Engineered products using smaller pieces of lumber were created to fill the gap. You must use engineered products in strict accordance with manufacturers' span specifications. In addition, you must install them with specified techniques and, in some cases, special connectors.

Glue-Laminated Lumber A glue-laminated beam is made up of smaller pieces of wood glued together lengthwise with waterproof glue. Glue-laminated lumber can be as long as you like—25 feet or longer. Each beam is specifically engineered to support an intended load. No matter what kind of glue-laminated lumber you install, you can't just nail it in place. You'll need framing connectors, shear plates, threaded rods, nail-on clips, or hangers at the connections.

Glue-laminated lumber is built up of finger-jointed dimensional lumber that must be sized for your application. The lumber is usually used as ridge beams, purlins, headers, and floor girders. Cambered beams are also available.

Laminated-Veneer Lumber (LVL). LVL can replace steel or an oversize glue-laminated beam. It is made, as the name implies, by laminating ¼-inch-thick plies together to a thickness of 4½ inches. You'll have to consult with the manufacturers' span charts to determine the size

Laminated-veneer lumber (LVL) is a beam composed of wooden plies (like the layers of a plywood panel) glued together. The beams can be ordered in depth from 9¼ to 18 in. and anything up to 60 ft. long.

LVL to use on your job. Even when you get the span rating down, be careful, because you can't notch or drill LVLs for pipes, wires, and heating or air-conditioning ducts, and you have to use the proper connectors.

Parallel-Strand Lumber Parallel-strand lumber is a kind of engineered beam, between 1¾ and 7 inches thick, made of thin strands of Douglas fir and/or southern yellow pine. The strands are glued together running parallel with one another. These beams are more dimensionally stable than LVLs or glue-laminated lumber beams, and they serve in the same applications. Parallel-strand lumber resists cupping and twisting when stored, which is a potential problem with some glue-laminated beams and LVLs.

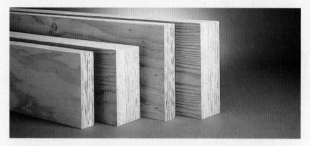

Parallel-strand lumber, similar to glue-laminated lumber, is made from individual strands of softwood lumber and an adhesive. These engineered beams may be up to 7 in. thick; you can order them in lengths up to 60 ft.

Wood I-Joists Wood I-joists are straight, dimensionally stable, and ideal for longer spans. I-joists are light and easy to install. The web, or center, of a wood I-joist is typically ½-inch plywood or oriented-strand board (OSB), and the 2-inch rails at the top and bottom are fir. Wood I-joists come in four sizes: 9½, 11⅞, 14, and 16 inches deep. Some connections may require special hardware.

Wood I-joists can replace lumber joists in floors and ceilings. They are made with solid- or engineered-wood rails (the edges of the I) and ½-in. plywood or OSB webs. Framing connectors may be required.

RATING PANEL PRODUCTS

When you purchase structural panels, a grading label tells you what you're buying. The leading grading association is the APA, The Engineered Wood Association, and you're most likely to see its stamp on panels.

Panel Grade. Panel products are rated in a number of categories. If you look at a typical APA grade stamp, you'll see the panel grade on the top line. This entry designates the proper application for the panel—rated sheathing, rated flooring, rated underlayment, and the like.

Span Rating. Next you'll see a large number or numbers, indicating the span rating. This rating is the recommended center-to-center spacing in inches of studs/joists/rafters over which you can place the panel. If you see numbers like 32/16, the left number shows the maximum spacing in inches of the panel when used in roofing—32 inches of allowable span with three or more supports—and the right number gives the maximum spacing when the panel is used as subflooring—16 inches of allowable span with three or more supports.

Thickness. The grade stamp also identifies the thickness of the panel—⅜ inch, ⁷⁄₁₆ inch, ¹⁵⁄₃₂ inch, ²³⁄₃₂ inch, and so on.

Exposure. The stamp also lists the exposure and durability classification for plywood. Exterior indicates exposure to weather is possible; Exposure 1 designates suitability for wall and roof sheathing; Exposure 2, for applications that will have low moisture exposure, such as subfloors.

Mill & Standards Numbers. The mill number simply identifies the manufacturer. The remaining numbers on the label—the national evaluation report (NER) and performance-rated panel standard (PRP)—indicate that the panel meets all construction requirements and requisite codes.

Veneer Grades. Plywood is also rated for veneer grades, and that rating appears on the edge of the plywood in combinations of letters. There are six categories in veneer ratings: N, A, B, C Plugged, C, and D, indicating descending order of quality. N is a smooth surface of select woods with no defects, but you won't be using N in framing. It's for use in cabinetry. For construction-grade plywood, the face-and-back-veneer grades are combinations of letters. B-C, for example, is suitable for sheathing, while you'd use A-B when both the face and back veneers will show. A-C or A-D is suitable when only the A side will show.

COMMON PLYWOOD TYPES

For most outbuilding projects you'll be using ½-inch or ⅝-inch BC or CDX plywood—Exposure 1 for wall and roof sheathing and Exposure 2 for subfloors. If you're finishing a barn or shed with plywood alone, you may want to consider AC, which has one "good" side without any repair plugs or major defects.

Another alternative is Texture 1-11, which has grooves cut into it to resemble board siding. T1-11 comes in 4 × 8-foot and larger panels. Stacking panels produces a seam that should be covered.

SMART TIP

When storing lumber at the work site, stack individual pieces so that air circulates around each piece. Keep the lumber off of the ground, and cover with a waterproof tarp.

TYPICAL PLYWOOD GRADE

Grade stamp information includes the panel's use, thickness, grade, exposure rating, and mill identification.

Fasteners
NAILS

The trick to choosing nails is to match the nail to the task. Codes often specify sizes of common nails for framing because they have an extra-thick shank and a broad head. You should use duplex, or double-headed, nails when you know you'll be removing the nail—in temporary sheathing, for example. Duplex nails allow you to snug the bottom nailhead up tight, but still give your hammer claw purchase to pull them out easily.

Besides common nails, you're likely to use ring-shank nails for subflooring; roofing nails and staples for applying felt paper, roofing shingles, and air-infiltration barriers (housewrap); and finishing nails for window- and door-jamb installations. Ring-shank nails have ridges on their shafts for extra holding power. Roofing nails have large heads to hold paper securely.

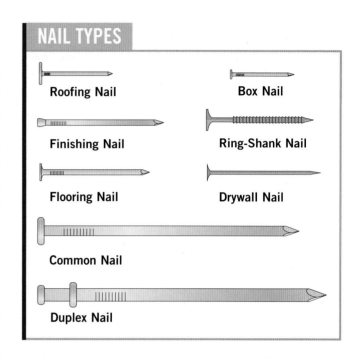

NAIL TYPES

Roofing Nail · Box Nail · Finishing Nail · Ring-Shank Nail · Flooring Nail · Drywall Nail · Common Nail · Duplex Nail

Finishing nails are thin, with small heads that you can easily drive beneath the surface of the wood with a nail set.

SCREWS

There are many types of screws, but you'll probably use only a few in a shed project: wood screws or deck (buglehead) screws for joining lumber, and lag screws for making heavy-duty wood-to-wood attachments. Lag screws, sometimes called lag bolts because of their bolt-like heads, are heavy-duty screws that you drive with a socket wrench. They have wide threads for biting into wood like a screw but a hex-shaped head like a bolt. Lag

Tips on Materials, Delivery, and Storage

Stage deliveries so that your materials aren't backlogged and you'll never run short of what you need. A good approach is to produce all your cut lists at the beginning of the job, break them down into work stages (foundation, rough framing, rafters, sheathing, roofing, windows and doors, siding and interior finish), and assign delivery dates for the materials needed for each work stage.

Using your site plan, with a clear outline of the footprint of your shed, designate some material drops. Lumber is heavy, so have it dropped close by. If you use trusses, which are fragile until set in place, don't schedule delivery until your truss crew is on hand. Windows and doors can go into a nearby garage. Trim lumber or siding should be set in a clean, dry area up on blocks.

Though it may be sunny and dry when materials are delivered, you should protect your deliveries against the elements. Many lumberyards have pallets that they will offer for free to keep the wood off the ground. Covering it with plastic is a good idea, but leave the ends of the wood open to breathe.

Finally, plan your deliveries to take advantage of any labor-saving tools the lumberyards offer. If the delivery truck has a lift, have them place lumber as close to the work site as possible.

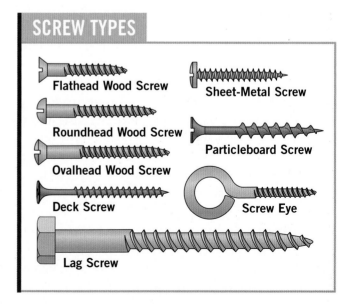

SCREW TYPES

Flathead Wood Screw · Sheet-Metal Screw · Roundhead Wood Screw · Particleboard Screw · Ovalhead Wood Screw · Deck Screw · Screw Eye · Lag Screw

Nail Sizes and Weights

Pennyweight	Length (in.)	Nails/lb. (Common)
2d	1	876
3d	1¼	568
4d	1½	316
5d	1¾	271
6d	2	181
7d	2¼	161
8d	2½	106
10d	3	69
12d	3¼	63
16d	3½	49
20d	4	31
30d	4½	24
40d	5	18
60d	6	14

screws are sized according to the diameter of their shanks: usually ⁵⁄₁₆, ⅜, or ½ inch.

Wood and deck screws are generally slotted or Phillips head, although there are others available. These screws are sized by their thickness, referred to by number. A screw's number indicates the diameter of its shank, the solid shaft of the screw measured at the base of the threads near the head. Common sizes are #6, #8, and #10. Of course, lengths can vary. A #8 screw, for example, can be nearly any length up to about 3½ inches. The heavier the gauge, the more likely you are to find it in longer lengths.

BOLTS

Bolts fall into three main categories: carriage bolts, machine bolts, and stove bolts. Specialty bolts add many more categories to the list and ones designed for specific functions. There are also about a dozen kinds of nuts and at least four kinds of washers. Each category of bolt, nut, and washer has a specific type of use.

You probably won't find many framing applications for machine bolts, which have hex- or square-shaped heads, and stove bolts, which have rounded heads with a slot for a screwdriver. But carriage bolts, which have unslotted oval heads, can be effective when attaching structural lumber face-to-face or major timbers to posts. Carriage bolts have a square shoulder just beneath the head that digs into the wood as you tighten the bolt, which prevents it from slipping and spinning in the hole, and they are sized according to the diameter of their shanks and their length.

Another bolt you're likely to use, the anchor bolt, attaches the sill plate to the top of a foundation of large sheds. Wedge-type bolts and J-bolts are the most common types.

2 Tools & Materials

SCREW SIZES

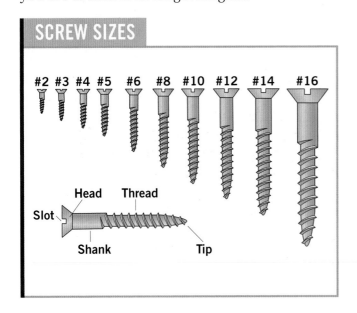

#2 #3 #4 #5 #6 #8 #10 #12 #14 #16

Slot · Head · Thread · Shank · Tip

BOLT TYPES

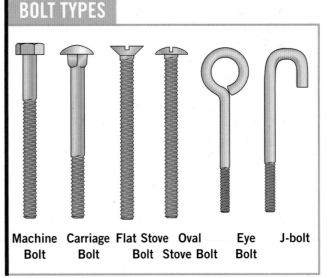

Machine Bolt · Carriage Bolt · Flat Stove Bolt · Oval Stove Bolt · Eye Bolt · J-bolt

3

Foundation Choices

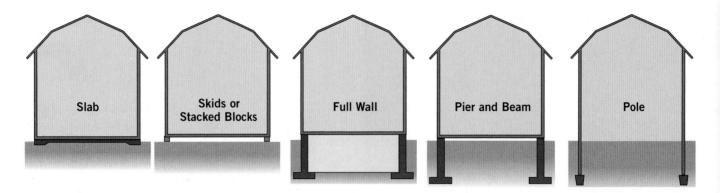

Slab   Skids or Stacked Blocks   Full Wall   Pier and Beam   Pole

Types of Foundations

Most sheds will not need a permanent foundation like the one you have on your house. In most cases, the foundations used on the five sheds we built for this book will serve adequately. Four of our sheds were constructed on stacked blocks, and one was built on pressure-treated timbers. However, local regulations in your area may require a more permanent foundation. So it is best to check with the building department before beginning construction.

BUILDING FOUNDATIONS

If you plan on building a different foundation type than the ones used on our sheds, there are a variety of choices from which to choose. For example, if building on heavy clay soil, a shed built on skids may make the job easier. A shed that requires a more stable foundation may require a concrete slab with footings.

The way you plan on using your new shed can determine which type of foundation is best. If you are going to use your shed for storing garden tools, blocks stacked on gravel pads will suffice. If the shed will be a workshop of some type, you may want a slab foundation. Or you may want to support the shed with poured concrete piers.

LAY OUT THE FOUNDATION

To lay out the rough corners of a basic building, you'll need four 2×4 stakes and a measuring tape. To find the location of your building's corners, measure from your property line or from an existing structure on your property. To make sure your layout is square, measure the diagonals (they will be the same length in a square or rectangle), or use the 3-4-5 triangulation method.

SQUARING CORNERS

Check to make sure corners of the foundation layout are square by using the 3-4-5 method of triangulation. Starting at corner A, measure 3 feet along one guideline, and mark point B. Starting again from corner A, measure 4 feet along the guideline perpendicular to the first one, and mark point C. Adjust the AC line until the distance BC is exactly 5 feet. Angle BAC is now a true 90-degree angle. You can double-check the squareness of corners and the overall layout by measuring the diagonals between opposite corners.

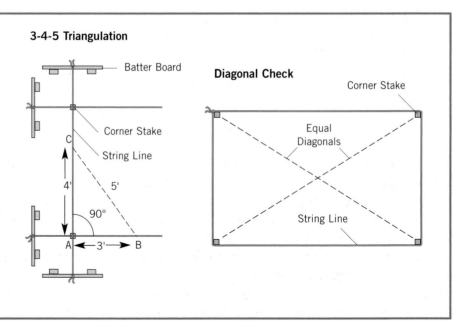

3-4-5 Triangulation

Batter Board
Corner Stake
String Line
C
4'
5'
90°
A ◄— 3' —► B

Diagonal Check

Corner Stake
Equal Diagonals
String Line

MAKING BATTER BOARDS

TOOLS
Circular saw
Clamps
Power drill-driver
Short sledgehammer
Spirit level
Line level
Measuring tape

Work gloves
Safety glasses

MATERIALS
2x4 stakes
1x4 boards
Drywall screws
Mason's string

1 Cut 16 stakes (four for each corner) from 2x4s, about 3 ft. long, with pointed ends. These stakes support the horizontal batter boards.

2 Set pairs of 2x4 stakes at roughly right angles to each other, 2 or more feet outside the corners and parallel with the lines of the foundation.

3 Make batter boards by cutting 2-ft. 1x4s. After drilling pilot holes, screw the batter boards to the stakes, using clamps to hold the boards in position.

4 Use a level to check the batter boards. This allows you to stretch level string lines along the perimeter of the building foundation.

5 Tack nails into the batter boards. Then fasten guidelines to the nails in the boards to establish the exact building corners and overall outline.

SMART TIP 3

Once you have outlined the base of the new shed, double-check that the location meets any setback requirements that apply.

Foundation Choices

To lay out large foundations, especially those being built on a slope, it's wise to use a transit level or builder's level.

If you're not going to excavate the area using heavy machinery, you can tie mason's string to nails on the corner boards and keep these lines as your layout marks. Once the layout is square, if the strings will get in your way, use spray paint to mark the ground beneath the lines. If you need to excavate the site, however, you'll need to build batter boards, which move the stakes outside of the building layout, a must if you will be excavating with heavy equipment. Otherwise, a bulldozer or backhoe will destroy your corner boards.

Treated-Timber Skids

Rot-resistant timber skids made of pressure-treated lumber can ably serve as a shed foundation. The timbers you select should be rated for ground contact. To facilitate drainage, the timbers should sit on a bed of ¾-inch gravel that is at least 6 inches deep. However, some building departments may require a deeper bed of gravel, especially in areas subject to frost heave.

The gravel bed under the timbers has to extend under all of the timbers used. Excavating this large area by hand can be a real chore. Consider hiring a landscaper to excavate the area and fill it to grade with gravel.

BUILDING A SKID FOUNDATION

TOOLS	MATERIALS
Shovel	Cloth or polyethylene sheeting
Circular saw	Pea gravel
Spirit level	Pressure-treated 4x4s or 6x6s

1 After laying out the outline of your shed on the ground, use a shovel to excavate out the first 4 or 5 in. of soil. Tamp the remaining subgrade firm with a hand tamper or the end of a 2x4.

Block Foundations

These foundations consist of blocks stacked on a base of ¾-inch gravel. Ideally, the gravel should extend below the frost line, especially in areas that are subject to frost heave. This type of foundation keeps excavation at a minimum. Simply dig a hole that accommodates the dimensions of the block plus a 6-inch border around the block. In most cases, a 4 to 6-foot spacing will suffice, but check requirements with your local building inspector.

With this type of foundation, it is the weight of the shed itself that holds the structure in place. However, many local codes now require steel anchors on sheds to prevent the shed from blowing over during periods of high winds. These anchors are driven through the shed's floor framing and into the ground.

Another option is to build a concrete footing and attach blocks to the footing with mortar. To attach the blocks to the framing of the shed, fill the hollow block with concrete, and install anchor bolts in the concrete before it sets.

2 Cover the hole with landscape fabric or 6-mil perforated polyethylene sheeting, and fill it in with gravel. This will help the drainage and keep the foundation timbers from rotting.

ABOVE Anchor bolts are set into the top course of block or into concrete. With a framing square, measure from the outside edge of the block or slab to the bolt; then mark that distance in from the sill's edge.

ABOVE Solid concrete blocks provide a good foundation for most garden sheds. For hilly sites, use the blocks to create a level base for the floor. A bead of construction adhesive will hold the stack in place.

3 Place two 4x4 or 6x6 timbers, pressure-treated and rated for ground contact, parallel with each other. Align their outer edges with the outer edges of the shed.

4 Check the timbers for level, and add or subtract gravel as needed. Use a straight 2x4 longer than the width of the shed to make sure that the timbers are level with each other.

SMART TIP 3

To minimize damage to your lawn from heavy equipment, use wheeled, compact excavators. Some feature tires that are lawn friendly.

Foundation Choices

Working with Concrete

Concrete is a mixture of portland cement, sand, gravel, and water. You can purchase the dry ingredients separately or buy them premixed, generally in 80-pound bags.

MIXING OPTIONS

For large-scale projects, however, you should order ready-mix concrete. It is sold by the cubic yard and delivered in a truck ready to pour. For smaller jobs—for example, form-tube piers for a small storage shed—you can mix your own concrete by adding water according to the instructions of the bag or by following the table, "Concrete Ingredients by Proportion," opposite.

But don't get too ambitious. One cubic yard, only enough for an 8 × 10-foot 4-inch slab, would require about 40 of those 80-pound bags. For mid-size jobs or those that a concrete truck can't drive to, it makes sense to rent a portable power mixer. For estimating purposes, you can make about 1 cubic yard of concrete with five 94-pound bags of portland cement, 14 cubic feet of sand, and 21 cubic feet of gravel.

ORDERING CONCRETE

Before you call, have an estimate for your order. Most ready-mix contractors will require only a day's notice. It's important to double-check your measurements of length times width times depth (and

MIXING CONCRETE	
TOOLS	**MATERIALS**
Mason's hoe	Concrete mix
Wheelbarrow	Water
Shovel	
Work gloves	

1 If concrete is too wet, ridges made in the mix with a trowel won't hold their shape. The concrete will be easy to mix and pour, but will not settle evenly nor provide its rated strength.

2 If concrete is too dry, you won't be able to make any ridges in the mix. It will be difficult to work. Mainly, the concrete will not cure properly and will not develop required strength.

3 When the concrete is mixed correctly, the ridges will hold most of their shape; only a little water will be visible on the surface. Place the concrete before it becomes too stiff.

CURING CONCRETE	
TOOLS	**MATERIALS**
Garden hose	Curing compound
Paint roller	Straw
	Tarpaulin/plastic sheeting

1 To keep concrete sufficiently moist during the curing process, you can periodically spray the finished surface lightly but thoroughly with water from a garden hose.

2 A chemical curing compound, applied to concrete with a paint roller or air-powered paint sprayer, is one way to prevent water loss during curing. Apply it after the surface has set up.

3 Another way to prevent concrete from drying prematurely is to cover the slab with plastic sheeting. Burlap or straw can also be used but must be kept moist.

your calculations) to specify the order in cubic yards. Always round up your numbers so that you don't run short of material.

MIX VARIATIONS

When hand-mixing, you may be tempted to adjust the mix proportions—say, by adding more water to make the concrete easier to mix and pour. However, as water content can drastically affect strength, the best policy is to order ready-mixed concrete or precisely follow directions on the bags.

Concrete Ingredients by Proportion

Maximum Size Course Aggregate Inches	Air-Entrained Concrete				Concrete without Air			
	Number of Parts per Ingredient				Number of Parts per Ingredient			
	Cement	Sand*	Coarse Aggregate	Water	Cement	Sand*	Coarse Aggregate	Water
⅜	1	2¼	1½	½	1	2½	1½	½
½	1	2¼	2	½	1	2½	2	½
¾	1	2¼	2½	½	1	2½	2½	½
1	1	2¼	2¾	½	1	2½	2¾	½
1½	1	2¼	3	½	1	2½	3	½

Note:7.48 gallons of water equals 1 cubic foot. One 94-pound bag of portland cement equals about 1 cubic foot.
*"Wet" sand sold for most construction use.
The combined finished volume is approximately two-thirds the sum of the bulk volumes.

The standard proportion of water to cement produces concrete with a compressive strength of 3,000 to 4,000 pounds per square inch (psi). Adding less water makes mixing more difficult and could weaken the mix.

Ready-mix concrete is also available with additives unavailable to the DIYer. One type produces microscopic air bubbles. This air-entrained concrete is more resistant to cracking than concrete you mix on site. There are also additives that accelerate the curing time for concrete poured in cold weather. You can order ready-mix concrete to a greater compressive strength than hand-mixed concrete, to support a greater building load.

CURING

The process of hardening concrete and bringing it to its full strength is called curing. Concrete begins to harden as soon as it is mixed and can support your weight within a few hours. Most of the curing takes place in the first two weeks, but it takes a month to reach near its peak hardness. The thicker the concrete, the more time it needs to cure completely. Most concrete needs to be kept moist over seven consecutive days above 50° F to cure properly. If the temperature is above 70° F, the concrete may cure in five days; high-early-strength concrete needs only three.

Curing concrete can be sprinkled periodically with water and covered with plastic sheeting, burlap, canvas, or straw to limit dehydration. There are also liquid curing compounds that you can roll onto concrete.

Curing in Extreme Heat. Concrete will dehydrate too quickly in hot weather, robbing it of the water it needs to cure. In extreme cases, a steady hot, dry breeze can accelerate evaporation so that the surface begins to set before it can be smoothed. There are some solutions, such as adding flaked ice or cooling down the aggregates with a sprinkler before adding them to the mix. To eliminate the risk of wasting your efforts on a job that is not going to last, don't pour in temperatures over 90°F. It's also important to remember that if the mix makes contact with a hot surface, moisture may burn off immediately. It's wise to spray some cool water on forms that are sitting in the sun as well as on the reinforcing bar, which can get quite hot to the touch.

SMART TIP **3**

Protect lawns from the wheels of your wheelbarrow by creating a path made of wide planks.

Foundation Choices

Piers & Posts

Concrete piers should be set into the ground every 6 to 8 feet under your shed. The shed's floor joists are attached to the piers with fasteners. This provides strong anchor points that tie the shed to the ground. Excavating for circular piers (which are often created by remain-in-place fiber forms) can be done by hand with a posthole digger. It's hard work, but you can rent a gas-powered posthole digger called a power auger. Note that gas-powered augers are hard to control (especially on sloped sites), and they take a great deal of strength to position and operate.

Piers can also be created by using the ground itself serving as a form; these are called "formless piers," but they do not work well in areas where there is sandy soil or heavy frost heaving. The photo sequence opposite provides step-by-step information on how to create formless piers.

SETTING PIERS WITH FORM TUBES

TOOLS

Posthole digger or power auger

Mason's hoe

Mason's trowel

Wheelbarrow or plywood

Spirit level

Hammer

Wrench

Work gloves

Handsaw

MATERIALS

Fiber tubes

J-Bolt

Concrete

1 Dig holes for your piers with a posthole digger or power auger to below the frost depth. Rocky or wooded soil will be difficult to work. Fill the bottom with 2 in. of gravel for support and drainage.

2 Insert a fiber form tube into the hole. It should protrude from the soil level about 6 in. Cut off any excess with a handsaw. Plumb the inside of the form with a spirit level to ensure straightness.

3 Check the form tube for plumb and level. Then backfill around the form with soil. Remove large rocks from the fill; small rocks can be added near the bottom of the hole.

4 Pour concrete from a wheelbarrow directly into the form. Before the concrete hardens, insert a J-bolt into the center, leaving the threads above the concrete surface.

5 After the concrete sets, attach post-base hardware using a washer and nuts. The post sits on a metal standoff that allows for drainage and keeps the bottom of the post dry.

SETTING FORMLESS PIERS

TOOLS	MATERIALS
Posthole digger or power auger	Steel reinforcing bar
Measuring tape	Post hardware
Shovel	
Wheelbarrow	
Spirit level	
Hammer	

1 Use a shovel and a posthole digger—or to save time, a rented power auger—to excavate a hole for a formless pier. The earthen walls of the hole serve as the formwork.

2 Measure the depth of the hole carefully to make sure that the base of the pier will rest on undisturbed or compacted soil that is below the minimum frost depth for your region.

3 Fill the hole with the required concrete mix and steel reinforcement bars. The bottom of the hole should be tamped down with a tamper or the end of a 2x4 or 4x4.

4 Insert a metal base for a post or girder into the concrete when the mix is just firm enough to hold it but not yet hardened. This hardware will attach the framing to the pier. The base keeps the bottom of the post from coming in contact with the ground.

5 Adjust the hardware so that it is level, plumb, and properly oriented to support the structural post or beam, which will be installed later. Once the concrete has set, it can't be adjusted.

SMART TIP 3

To deal with large piles of gravel, spread out sheets of 6-mil polyethyle and dump the gravel on the sheets. Gravel placed on the lawn is hard to clean up.

Foundation Choices

Concrete Footings

For larger structures and in areas subject to frost heave, footings are the first step to a complete perimeter wall foundation or floor slab. (Some slabs are monolithic, which means that both footing and slab are poured at once.)

ASSEMBLING THE FORMS

Using your batter boards and strings as guides, dig the footing to the required width and depth. In some cases, part of the footing may extend above grade. If the soil is loose at the bottom of the trench, compact it with a tamper to prevent the concrete from settling. If you remove large rocks, fill the depressions and tamp them down firmly.

Drive stakes for the forms 18 to 24 inches apart. Clamp on the form boards before fastening them. Attach 1×2 braces across the top of the forms every 2 feet or so to keep them from spreading when you pour the concrete. To keep cracks from forming, place steel reinforcing bars (#4 rebar) horizontally. You may need several rows for deep footings. Before you pour the concrete, double-check to make sure the form boards are level and plumb.

POURING THE CONCRETE

Pour or shovel wet concrete into the forms, flush to the top. As you pour, use a shovel or mason's hoe to work out any air pockets. Use a wood float, flat trowel, or short length of 2×4 to smooth the top surface of the footing. After smoothing and leveling the concrete, set anchor bolts into the concrete 1 foot from the ends of each wall and 6 feet on center. The bolts are used to secure the sill plate that anchors the structure to the foundation. If the footing will support a block wall, you'll need to add vertical rebars to tie the wall to the footing.

BUILDING FOOTING FORMS

TOOLS	MATERIALS
Power drill with screwdriver bit	Concrete
Mason's twine	Gravel
Shovel	Two-by formwork boards
4' spirit level	2x4 stakes
Measuring tape	1x4 batter boards
Hammer	Duplex nails
Clamps	Galvanized screws
Short sledgehammer	Plywood gussets
	Form oil or motor oil

1 After setting up batter boards and marking the perimeter, begin excavating the soil within your string lines. Remember, the footings must reach below the local frost-depth line.

2 Drive in the stakes to support the form boards. You can build them from 1x4s or 2x4s with an angle cut to form the tip. Most footings are twice the width of the wall.

3 Use a clamp to fasten the form boards to the stakes temporarily. Check the boards for level; adjust them as needed; and then nail or screw the boards to the stakes.

4 Secure any butt joints in the formwork with ½-in.-thick plywood gussets. Use a power drill and 1½-in. screws to fasten these in place across the exterior face of each joint.

5 Use 1x2 spreaders to bridge the forms every few feet. These braces ensure that the weight of the concrete as it is poured will not cause the forms to bulge.

BUILDING CONCRETE FOOTINGS

TOOLS
Pliers
Hacksaw
Wire cutters
Mason's hoe
Wheelbarrow

Shovel
Mason's trowel
2x4 screed

MATERIALS
Rebar
Tie wire

Bricks, blocks, or wire chairs
Plywood gussets
Screws
Concrete
Anchor bolts

1 Support rebar at the proper height at least an inch or two off the ground—with pieces of brick. Wire supports called chairs work better than bricks if you can find them.

2 Secure the rebar to the chairs or supports with wire ties, twisted tightly with pliers. This keeps the supports from being forced out of position by the concrete during the pour.

3 You'll need to bend the rebar around corners. Adjoining pieces of rebar should be lapped by several inches to provide unbroken support. Secure the laps together with wire ties.

4 Transport the concrete to the formwork using a wheelbarrow, bucket, or other container, and pour it into place. Use a shovel to distribute the concrete evenly throughout the form.

5 Fill the forms completely, using a hoe or shovel to spread it around evenly. Tamp the concrete as you work in order to eliminate any voids or air bubbles, particularly in corners.

6 Once the footing has cured, use a mason's trowel to fill corners, working along the inside edges of the form boards.

7 Use a 2x4 screed board, cut a few inches longer than the total width of the footing, to fill the forms evenly and strike off any excess concrete above the level of the formwork.

8 Embed steel anchor bolts (for sills) or rebar (for block walls) into the concrete at 6 ft. on center and within 1 ft. of each corner or door opening.

SMART TIP **3**

Concrete forms are meant to be removed once the concrete cures. Make the job easier by building the forms with duplex nails and coating the form boards with motor oil for easy removal.

Foundation Choices

POURING A SLAB

TOOLS	MATERIALS
Compactor	Rebar
Mason's twine	Tie wire
Measuring tape	Duplex nails
Line level	Two-by form boards
Rebar chairs	
Shovel	2x4 or 1x4 stakes
Sledgehammer	Welded or woven-wire mesh
Wheelbarrow	
Broom	Bricks, blocks, or wire chairs
Screed	
Float	Wire ties
Edging trowel	Gravel
Jointing trowel	

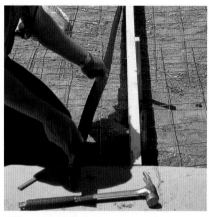

1 To strengthen the concrete, lay welded wire within the slab, generally on short supports called chairs. You can also use bricks or rocks to keep the wire above the soil.

2 If the slab will also be the finished floor, control joints will hide any cracks in the bottom of the joint. They can be formed into the pour or cut with a concrete saw after the slab hardens.

3 After you have evenly distributed the concrete throughout the form, you'll use a screed board to strike off the excess and fill in the hollows. Use a 2x4 slightly longer than the width of the slab.

4 As concrete pours from the ready-mix truck, use hoes and shovels to spread it evenly throughout the slab forms. You'll need several helpers to do this while the mix is still plastic.

5 Depending on the slab's use, you can smooth (with a float) the rough surface left by screeding (such as for a floor slab) or texture it with a broom for better traction (for a patio).

ESTIMATING CONCRETE FOR SLABS

Square Feet

Cubic Feet / Cubic Yards

4" THICK
5" THICK
6" THICK
7" THICK
8" THICK

To figure out how much concrete to mix or order, you can use the chart at left. If you prefer, total up the volume inside the forms in cubic feet (length x height x width); then divide this figure by 27 to convert it into the ordering standard of cubic yards. To avoid a shortfall, it's smart to build in a reasonable excess factor of about 8 percent by changing the conversion factor to 25. Remember that an 80-pound bag of concrete mix will make only two-thirds of a cubic foot. Large orders measured in cubic yards will require a rented power mixer (and many bags of premixed concrete) or delivery from a concrete truck.

Concrete Slabs

The concrete slab, often called a slab-on-grade (the grade being the surface of the ground), is a monolithic piece of concrete, usually 4 to 6 inches thick, poured onto the ground over a bed of gravel within forms. Local codes specify the thickness of slabs for different purposes.

Soil preparation beneath a slab is crucial. Before you form a slab, prepare the soil to ensure proper drainage around and beneath it. In cold climates, this might mean replacing the soil to 50 percent of the frost depth with gravel. In some parts of the country, a polyethylene vapor barrier should be placed between the soil and the gravel base.

FORMWORK

Around the edges, a slab is formed by boards: 2×6s, 2×8s, 2×10s, 2×12s, or a combination of these. Use 2×4 scab boards to hold the form boards together as you place them around the perimeter. Be careful to keep them plumb: check periodically with a spirit level. Brace and stake the boards in place using 2×2s or 2×4s, either driven into the ground or run diagonally as kickers. Also use a water level or transit to check that the forms are level across their tops.

When positioning the slab form boards, use mason's string as a guide. A batter-board system (page 55) for defining form placement works well and provides a precise string outline to follow when forming the slab perimeter.

SLAB CONSTRUCTION

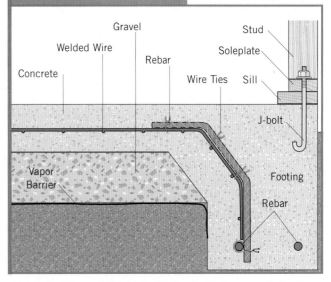

Concrete slabs need to be built on a bed of compacted soil and 4 to 6 in. of gravel. Rebar and welded-wire mesh add strength and tie the thinner slab to the thicker footings.

REINFORCEMENT

You must reinforce concrete slabs with steel rods called rebar and welded-wire mesh. Within footings, you lay #4 rebar, and in the main area of the slab itself use #10 reinforcing mesh. The rebar will also serve as an anchor for the J-bolts, which hold the sill plates in place once the concrete dries and you start framing. (You can also place the J-bolts in the wet concrete.) Most codes call for J-bolts no more than 6 feet apart.

SLAB FOOTINGS

Most slabs are thicker around their outside perimeters to carry the load of the structure. This thicker section is called the footing. The footing and slab are integrally one piece of concrete, poured at the same time. To create the footing, dig deeper where you want the footing so that more concrete can be poured into the excavation. If you have unstable soil, use 2×8s or 2×10s to form the sides of the footing.

Construction Gravel Basics

Gravel is commonly used beneath foundations, footings, piers, and slabs because it doesn't retain water and therefore helps defeat frost heaving. The most commonly used gravel for this purpose is ¾ gravel ("three-quarter gravel"). This means that the individual stones are a maximum ¾ inch diameter. Gravel is available as small as ¼ inch in diameter.

Other types of construction stone include pea gravel—which is made up of round, smooth stones—and crushed stone, which provides a stable base because the rock surfaces interlock with one another.

SMART TIP 3

Build slabs over a base of compacted gravel. For best results, rent a power tamper. Use it on the soil base and then on the gravel level.

Foundation Choices

Building Practices

Floor Framing

Framing houses and other large structures requires a great deal of specialized information dealing with sizing lumber to account for "live" and "dead loads." The requirements for simple sheds—those in the 8 × 10-foot-size range—are not as stringent. You will build a sturdy, long-lasting structure if you use 2×6 joists and rafters, and 2×4 studs. In most cases, there is no need to top windows and doors with beefed-up headers, but you should always check with the local building inspector before starting work.

For floors, create a frame the size of the perimeter of the building using joist stock and adding joists every 16 inches on center in the interior of the frame. For most of the sheds in this book, this type of floor simply rests on the foundation blocks. The weight of the structure keeps it in place. However, some municipalities require ground anchors to hold the shed on its foundation. The steel anchors are driven through the framing and into the ground. For building a shed on a concrete foundation, see "Frame on Foundation," below.

FRAME ON FOUNDATION

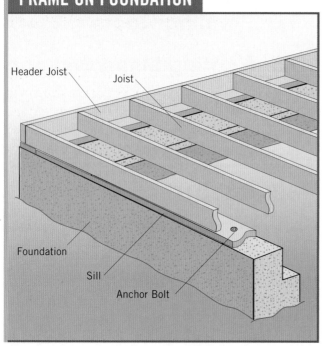

Basic floor framing is made up of header, or rim, joists and a grid of floor joists set at 16 or 24 in. on center that rests on foundation sills. Long spans may require a girder at midspan.

FRAMING THE FLOOR

TOOLS
Circular saw or hand saw
Framing square
Framing hammer
Measuring tape
Combination square
Bar clamp (if needed)

MATERIALS
Two-by lumber for joists and bridging
16d and 12d common nails
Joist hangers and joist-hanger nails (optional)
Carpenter's pencil

2 Tack the joists in place, and stop to check the perimeter frame to make sure it's square. Use a framing square at the corners, and measure the overall diagonals, which should be equal.

4 Mark your layout on opposite headers using 16-in. on-center marks, depending on the span and load. You may want to make duplicate layouts on both boards before installing them.

1 Place the rim joists on top of the sill (with both slab and wall foundations) or the beam (on pier foundations for a small shed as shown here).

3 End-nail the rim joists and end joist together with three 16d common nails. Check that they are tight against the sill. You may want to predrill nail holes near the ends to prevent splitting.

5 Once they are square, you can end-nail the joists through the rim joist with three 12d common nails. Local codes generally require that you set joists into metal joist hangers.

Installing the Subfloor

With the floor joists in place, it's time to put down the subfloor, or floor deck. In houses, the subfloor forms the base for floor coverings, such as carpet or finished wood, and is often covered with another layer of material, called underlayment, before finish materials are installed. In sheds and other utility buildings, you'll probably leave the subfloor unfinished.

MATERIALS

Generally a subflooring is ½-inch CDX plywood. If codes permit, you may also use waferboard, oriented-strand board (OSB), or other sheet materials. But in an outbuilding that isn't heated or cooled, use an exterior-grade material that can stand up to moisture. If you plan to store heavy tools and machinery, use ¾-inch plywood or two layers of ½-inch plywood.

INSTALLATION

You can nail plywood decking, but for maximum strength apply a bead of construction adhesive to the tops of the joists, and fasten the sheets with screws. Lay the subfloor by staggering panel edges so that the seams don't line up across the floor. If you start the first row with a full panel, start the second with a half panel. In an outbuilding where you anticipate a wet floor from tracking in and out, you might leave a ¹⁄₁₆-inch gap between panels to prevent the panels from buckling.

Nail or screw the subflooring every 12 inches along the edges and in the field of the plywood. If you don't use adhesive, nail or screw every 6 inches on the outside edges and 10 inches in the field. Remember that basic ½-inch sheets may satisfy local codes but may bend under the weight of a heavy lawn mower or other tools.

SMART TIP **4**

Keep your framing square handy. Use it as you work to check that the framing components are square.

Building Practices

INSTALLING A SUBFLOOR

TOOLS

Caulking gun
Hammer or power drill with screwdriver bit
Circular saw or table saw
Measuring tape
Chalk-line box
2-lb. sledgehammer

MATERIALS

Plywood or OSB panels
Subfloor adhesive
8d ring-shank nails or 2-in. deck screws

1 Although it is not a requirement, gluing down the subfloor will increase the floor's stiffness and decrease nail popping. Run a ¼-in.-dia. bead of subfloor adhesive down each joist.

2 Nail panels to the joists with 8d nails, spaced every 6 in. along the edge and every 10 in. elsewhere. Install panels with the face-grain perpendicular to the joists and stagger panel joints.

3 If you're using ordinary square-ended panels instead of tongue-and-groove subflooring, leave about a ¹⁄₁₆-in. space between the panels to allow for expansion without buckling.

4 If you started with a half panel in your first course, start the second course with a full panel. This keeps the panel seams from aligning over one joist and makes for a stronger floor.

5 You can use a scrap board, such as a 2x4, to work a panel into position. But this technique is more often used to fit together sheets of interlocking tongue-and-groove plywood.

Wall Framing

Stick-built walls are constructed on a modular system designed to provide a combination of structural strength and nailing surfaces for sheathing materials inside and out. Adding windows and doors generally requires extra studs because the openings don't normally fall exactly into the modular plan.

The base of the wall is a horizontal 2×4 (or a 2×6 in some cases) called a soleplate, or shoe. Studs sit on the shoe, generally every 16 inches on center. The top of the wall is capped with two more horizontal 2×4s called a top plate.

There are three kinds of studs in most walls. Full-height studs, sometimes called king studs, run from the soleplate to the top plate. Jack studs, also called trimmer studs, run from the shoe up alongside a full stud at rough openings. The top of the jack stud rests under the header over a window or door. Cripple studs are short 2×4s that fill in the spaces above and below a rough opening, for example, from the soleplate to the sill of a window. They are spaced to maintain the modular layout and provide nailing surfaces for siding and drywall or other surface materials.

ASSEMBLING THE WALL

Start by marking the plate and shoe according to the wall layout in your plans. Then you can cut the studs. A power miter box makes this job go quickly. King studs will be full length—generally 91½ inches for 8-foot ceilings. Jack studs will be king-stud length minus the combined height of the header and cripples above. You can cut the cripples and sills to length after you put the jack studs and headers in place. Some builders prefer to build rough openings after the wall has been raised.

One efficient way to build walls is to assemble the components on the deck and tip them into position. On long walls you'll need some help raising the structure, and on all walls you have to plan the framing carefully before nailing through the shoe and first plate and into the ends of the studs.

SQUARING THE WALL

Check walls to make sure they're square before you stand them in place, and again after you raise them. You can check the diagonals, which should be

WALL FRAMING

Double Top Plate
Cripple Stud
Wall Stud
Window Header
Door Header
Full Stud
Jack Stud
Window Sill
Jack Stud
Full Stud
Full Stud
Cutout
Jack Stud
Cripple Stud
Soleplate
Subfloor

A stick-framed wall consists of studs—vertical 2x4s or 2x6s—between a single horizontal soleplate, often called a shoe, and a double top plate. Windows and doors have framed headers and extra jack and cripple studs to account for the missing full studs.

equal if the wall is square. It also helps to lock up the position by tacking diagonal braces along the wall. Some builders also install sheathing before raising, although this makes the wall even heavier.

RAISING THE WALL

Before erecting any wall, snap a chalk line along the subfloor or slab to establish a reference guide for positioning the inside edge of the wall sole-plate. On a subfloor, also nail a few 2×4 cleats to the outside of the header joist to keep the wall from slipping off the deck as you raise it. With as many helpers as you need, slide the wall into position so that when you raise it, it will stand close to the guideline. Erect the wall, and align it to the chalk line.

Using a 4-foot spirit level, get the wall as close to plumb as possible. You'll fine-tune it for plumb when you install the adjacent wall. Run braces from studs to cleats that are nailed into the subfloor or on corners, to the outsides of the floor joists. When the wall is plumb, have a helper nail the braces to the cleats. With the bottom soleplate properly positioned, nail into the rim joists and floor joists with 16d nails. You can plumb a small wall by yourself. The

Laying Out the Walls

To lay out the soleplate and top plates of a wall, first cut a pair of straight 2x4s (or 2x6s) to length. Tack the soleplate to the subfloor and set the top plate flush against it. Make your first mark ¾ inch short of your on-center spacing (15¼ inches), and make an X past that mark. This will place center of the first stud 16 inches from the corner. Measure down the length of the plates, and mark where the common, full-length studs will fall, every 16 or 24 inches, and mark each of these studs with an X. You can also measure and mark the locations of cripple studs (C) and jack studs (O).

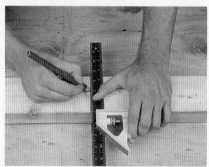

Avoid layout confusion by marking the shoe and the top plate the same way in a step-ahead system. You may want to mark the soleplate and top plate at the same time with a combination square.

Once the square line is drawn, step ahead of the line to mark the location of a stud with an X. You can also use the tongue of a framing square, which is 1½ inches wide, to mark the full width.

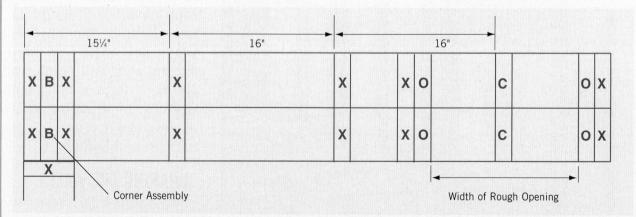

Corner Assembly

Width of Rough Opening

Lay out corners and rough openings on your plates as indicated on your plans. Mark all full-length studs with an X, jack studs (also called trimmers) with an O, blocking with a B, and cripples with a C.

WALL BRACING

To brace a corner, lock it in place with a 2x4. Leave the brace in place until the whole wall is finished—nail it outside the frame so it's out of the way.

Apply a spring brace to fix a bow in a stud wall. Nail a flat brace (at least 8 ft. long) to cleats on the floor and wall, and force the wall into plumb.

trick is to nail an angled brace to a cleat on the deck and clamp it to the wall. Check with a level, adjust and reclamp as needed, and tack the brace to hold the wall plumb. On long walls of 20 feet or so, brace each corner and several interior studs.

To check for plumb, hold a 4-foot level against a straight 2×4. Pay particular attention to corners. If the wall is leaning in or out, release any braces and adjust the wall. Apply force to the braces to push the wall out. To bring the wall in, attach a flat brace between two cleats (one attached to the wall and one to the floor) and use a two-by as a kicker to bow the brace and force the wall inward. You can also apply braces staked outside the building. Retack the braces to hold the wall in its proper position.

TOP PLATES

When adjoining walls are in proper position you can add the second top plate and tie the walls together. The top plate on one wall overlaps the bottom plate of the adjoining wall. Where partitions join exterior bearing walls, the top plate of the partition should lap onto the top plate of the exterior wall. Secure all laps with at least two 16d nails.

STUD CONFIGURATIONS AT CORNERS

If you plan on finishing the interior of your shed, you will need to provide a nailing base at the corners for the finish material. Stud-and-block corners use the most material, but they are the most

rigid. The three-stud corner saves time and a little material because you don't need the blocking. The two-stud corner is fine for a small shed with unfinished interior walls.

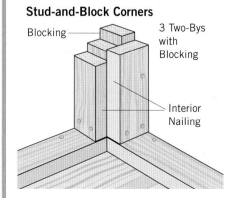

Stud-and-Block Corners
Blocking
3 Two-Bys with Blocking
Interior Nailing

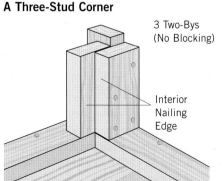

A Three-Stud Corner
3 Two-Bys (No Blocking)
Interior Nailing Edge

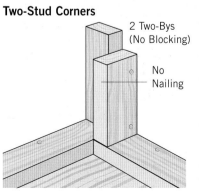

Two-Stud Corners
2 Two-Bys (No Blocking)
No Nailing

FRAMING WALLS

TOOLS
Carpenter's pencil
Circular saw or table saw
Combination square
Framing square
4-ft. spirit level
Hammer
Measuring tape
Safety goggles and work gloves

MATERIALS
2x4 or 2x6 lumber
16d and 12d common nails

1 Start by marking the layout on both the soleplate and one of the two top plates at the same time—this ensures that the studs will line up when the wall is erected and squared.

2 Work on the subfloor (or the surface of the slab) to assemble the frame. Position each stud; stand on it to prevent shifting; and nail through the soleplate with two 16d common nails.

3 When the soleplate is nailed on, shift to the top of the wall, and follow the same procedure to nail on one of the top plates. Before nailing, check the stud position for square.

4 Check the overall frame by comparing diagonal measurements. If the wall is square, the diagonals should be equal. Nail on a temporary brace.

5 Small shed walls can be raised by one person; larger walls may require three or more. The wall components are nailed to the floor framing with 16d nails and then braced.

6 Once the wall is braced, use a 4-ft. level to check several studs for plumb. It's easiest to assemble corner posts that may include short pieces of blocking on the deck and add them later.

7 With the walls straightened and the corner posts in place, you can install the second top plate, also called the cap plate. Stagger the joints over the corner in order to tie one wall to another.

8 Nail on the cap plate with 12d or 16d nails. Once all the exterior walls are in place, you can add sheathing and remove the temporary bracing as you nail on the sheets.

Windows & Doors

Stud placement is crucial for rough openings in walls where you insert doors and windows. The rough opening size is listed in window and door catalogs, and generally allows ½ to ¾ inch of shimming space around the unit. This allows you to plumb and level the window or door even when the adjacent wall frame is out of kilter. Each side of the opening has a full-height stud. Inside that stud is a shorter jack stud. The distance jack to jack, allowing for shimming space, is the rough opening.

On windows, a short jack stud helps to support the sill. You add a jack stud that runs from the sill up to the header. On most sheds, there is no need to install a beefy header above the window as shown below, simply frame the opening with 2×4s, but check with the building inspector for requirements in your area.

On doors, you need two long jack studs that run from the floor to the header, with cripple studs above. You can rest the jacks on the soleplate, or run them down to the plywood deck. This covers the shoe end grain and on exterior doors will bear on the joist or rim joist below.

BUILDING ROUGH OPENINGS

TOOLS
Circular saw
Combination square
Hammer
4-ft. spirit level
Measuring tape
Pencil
Safety goggles

MATERIALS
2x4 or 2x6 studs
Two-by headers
Common nails

1 At each side of the rough opening, nail a jack stud into the soleplate and adjacent full-height stud. In 2x4 walls, use two 10d nails every foot or so for stability.

2 Continue additional jack stud sections along both sides of the window opening. These framing members will help to support the weight carried by the header across the opening.

3 Make up a header with two 2x6s, sandwiching a sheet of ½-in. plywood that packs out the header to the wall thickness. Wider openings will require larger headers.

4 Add cripple studs above the header and below the sill to maintain the on-center layout of the wall. You need the cripples for nailing surfaces (and strength) under surface materials.

Framing Roofs

Though this section of the book will provide detailed rafter cutting instructions, along with the basic geometry required for calculating rafter length, you probably won't need all this information. Here's why: in the project sections of this book, we will show how to build sheds that are relatively small. Someone with even limited carpentry experience can easily calculate the angles where the rafter meets the top plate on a wall and the ridge beam. You can cut and trim just one rafter until it fits snugly, and then use this rafter as a "master" to mark and cut the remaining rafters.

Roofing Measurements

If you know the slope of a roof but don't know the total rise, you can determine that dimension using the total run on a symmetrical roof. First, divide the span in half to get the total run. Let's say your structure has a span of 20 feet. The total run is 10 feet. Now multiply the unit rise by the number of feet in the total run. An 8-in-12 roof with a total run of 10 feet means the total rise is 80 inches (8 × 10) or 6 feet 8 inches. If you increase the run, the slope doesn't change, but the total rise increases. For example, if you have a 12-foot run with an 8-in-12 roof, the total rise is 96 inches (8 × 12) or 8 feet.

When you determine rise, you use a measurement along a line from the cap plate's top outside edge to the ridge's centerline. The point at which the rafter measuring line and the ridgeboard centerline intersect is known as the theoretical ridgeboard height. The rise is the distance from the plate to the theoretical ridgeboard height.

But if math is not your strong point, there is another option. You erect braced posts at each end of the ridge, adjust the ridge up or down as needed with clamps, and test rafters for length, angle, and end cuts. This may be the best system for do-it-yourselfers working on an addition and trying to match an existing roof line. (See "Installing the Ridgeboard & Rafters," page 81.)

ROOF MEASUREMENTS

Ridgeboard · Common Rafter · Rafter Bay · Top Plate · Measuring Line · Gable-End Rafter · Run · Span · Collar Tie · Rise · Overhang · Theoretical Ridge Height · Centerline of Ridge

Roof Terminology

Rise is the height of the roof at its ridge measured from the top plate of the end wall below the ridge.

Span is the horizontal distance from wall to wall. A roof's span does not include the overhang at the eaves.

Run is the horizontal distance from one wall to a point under the ridge, or typically half the span.

Pitch is the angle of a roof as a ratio of the rise to the span. A 24-foot-wide structure, for example, with a gable roof that rises 10 feet from side wall to ridgeboard has a pitch of 10/24 or 5/12. A pitch of 1/4 or 1/3 is common for gable roofs. A Cape Cod–style roof might have a 1/2 pitch.

Slope is expressed as the rafter's vertical rise in inches, or unit rise, per 12 inches of horizontal run, or unit run. If a slope has a unit rise of 4 and a unit run of 12, the roof surface rises 4 inches for every 12 inches along the run line. This is expressed as 4:12 or 4 in 12. On most building plans, you'll notice a right triangle off to the side—for example, 4 in 12 with a 12 at the top of the triangle on one leg of the right angle and a 4 on the other leg. The hypotenuse of the triangle shows you the angle of slope. The higher the number of inches in unit rise, the steeper the roof. A 12-in-12 roof, common in Cape Cod-style roofs, rises a foot in elevation for every foot of run (a 45-degree angle).

SMART TIP   **4**

If you plan on having more than one shed or out-building in your yard, make sure they all have the same roof style to achieve a harmonious overall appearance.

Building Practices

Gable Framing

Calculating rafter length and the angles at the ridge and rafter tail is more complex than framing walls. But the job is doable using only basic math if you break down the task into smaller, more simple steps. On gable roofs, you can either run the rafters individually to a center ridgeboard or assemble gable-style trusses on the ground and lift them into position. Some lumberyards carry prefabricated trusses for several basic roof spans and pitches.

MEASURING GABLE RAFTERS

Because all common rafters in a gable roof are the same, you can mark and cut one, test the fit, and use it as a template.

Three Basic Cuts. Most common rafters get three cuts: a plumb cut at the ridge where the rafter rests against the ridgeboard; a plumb cut at the tail, which makes the shape of the bottom end; and a bird's-mouth cut where the rafter seats on the plate of the outside wall. Sometimes you need a fourth cut, a horizontal cut at the tail, which is often used with an overhang and soffit.

The simplest way to mark these cuts is to hold the lumber up to the ridgeboard, which you can temporarily install on vertical supports. Once the rafter is aligned with the top of the ridgeboard at one end and resting against the top plate at the other, you can scribe the ridge cut and the seat cut directly onto the rafter.

You can also measure these cut lines using a framing square. If you've stepped off the rafter, the first mark you make will be your plumb or ridge cut, the cut that rests against the ridgeboard.

Number of Rafters. If it's not included on your plans, you'll need to calculate the total number of rafters you'll need. For 16-inch-on-center framing, multiply the length of the building by three-quarters, and add 1 (L 3 0.75 + 1 = X rafters). For 24-inch-on-center framing, multiply the building length by one-half and add 1 (L 3 0.5 + 1 = Y rafters). If your plans include a gable-end overhang to match the eaves overhang, you'll need to add four pieces of lumber for the barge, or fly, rafters that extend beyond the gable-end walls.

Estimating the Size. Before you order rafter lumber, you must know what size boards to get. You can approximate the sizes using a framing

Three Methods for Calculating Rafter Length

There are three ways to calculate rafter length, aside from the trusted do-it-yourself method of holding a board in place and marking the cuts. The calculations used here are an example and are not meant for all rafters, but you can use the principles for any common gable rafter.

#1: Using the Pythagorean Theorem

Determine the roof slope. Here, assume a slope of 8 in 12, which means the roof rises 8 inches for every 12 inches it runs. Then determine the building width. For this example, assume the building is 30 feet wide. Next, determine the run. The run is one-half the building's width, in this case, 15 feet. Finally, determine the rise. Once you know the slope and run, you know the roof will rise 10 feet (8 x 15 = 120 inches, or 10 feet).

You're now ready to figure the rafter length for an 8-in-12 roof on a building 30 feet wide. If you think of half the roof as a right triangle, you already know the base (15) and altitude (10). You need to figure the hypotenuse of this right triangle, which represents the rafter length. Using the Pythagorean theorem:

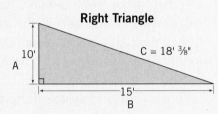

Right Triangle

$$A^2 + B^2 = C^2$$
$$10^2 + 15^2 = C^2$$
$$100 + 225 = 325$$
$$\sqrt{325} = 18.03$$

The square root of 325 feet is 18.03 feet, which equals 18 feet ⅜ inch. If your rise and/or run are not in whole feet but in feet and inches, then convert the whole figure to inches; do the math; and convert it back to feet. Use decimals of a foot rather than inches when you divide the resulting number of inches by 12 on a calculator to arrive at feet.

#2: Using a Rafter Table

The rafter table found on a framing square contains work-saving data and is useful for many calculations. You need only look at

the first line of the table, which gives unit rafter length for common gable rafters. To find the unit length you need, look on the blade below the inch designation that corresponds to your slope. If, for example, you're framing a 6-in-12 roof, look at the number below the 6-inch mark on the framing square's blade. You'll find it reads 13.42. If your total run is 14, multiply 13.42 by 14 to get 187.88 inches. Divide 187.88 by 12 to get 15.656 feet, or 15 feet 7⅞ inches.

#3: Stepping Off with a Framing Square

You can also accurately measure a rafter by stepping off dimensions with a framing square in 12-inch units of run.

Lay a straight piece of rafter stock across two sawhorses. Sight down the edge of the rafter, and position yourself on the crowned side, which will be the top of the rafter. To make accurate marking easier, attach adjustable stops called stair nuts or stair buttons to the square to set the rise and run positions.

Let's say you want to lay out a roof with an 8-in-12 slope. Lay the square on the left end of the stock. Hold the square's tongue in your left hand and its blade in your right. Pivot the square until the edge of the stock near you aligns with the unit rise mark (8 inches in this example) on the outside of the tongue and the 12-inch mark on the outside of the blade. Mark along the outside edge of the tongue for the ridge plumb line. You'll use this mark as the reference line for stepping off full 12-inch units.

If the span is an odd number of feet, say 25, with a run of 12½ feet, you'll have to include a half-step to accommodate the extra length. Mark off the partial step first, and then go on to step off full 12-inch units. Holding the square in the position in which you had it to mark the ridge cut, measure and mark the length of the odd unit along the blade.

Shift the square to your right along the edge of the stock until the tongue is even with the mark you just made. Mark off a plumb line along the tongue of the square. When you begin stepping off full units, remember to start from the new plumb line and not from the ridge cut line.

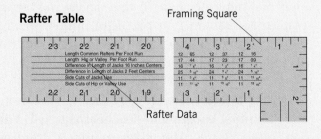

Rafter Table

Framing Square

Rafter Data

Rafter Layout

Partial Step

Framing Square

Rafter

square and measuring tape. To determine the exact rafter lengths, you can use any of three methods: work with rafter tables; use the Pythagorean theorem; or step off the rafters with a square.

To mark rafters, you have to find the roof slope indicated on the building plans. The rafter length will be determined by the roof slope and the building width. The rafter-length measurement will determine where you'll make the cuts on the rafters. The rafter length is the distance from the ridge to the edge of the building. Remember that the rafter size (and wood species and grade) will have to be approved by your local building department.

Subtracting the Ridgeboard Thickness. You start by calculating the length of the rafter to the center of the ridgeboard. Then you must shorten the rafter to accommodate the width of the board. Measure back from the center of the ridge line a distance of one-half the thickness of the ridgeboard. If you're using a two-by ridgeboard, the distance will be ¾ inch. Mark another plumb line at this point as the cut line.

Calculating the Overhang. The overhang (sometimes called projection) is the level distance from the edge of the building. But the actual rafter length is longer because of its slope. You can use the Pythagorean theorem to figure out the dimension you'll have to add to the rafter length for the overhang. If you want an 18-inch overhang on the same 8-in-12 roof, for example, you must envision the overhang area as a miniature roof. The run is 18 inches (the horizontal dimension of the overhang) and the rise is 12 inches ($8 \times 1.5 = 12$). Therefore,

$$12^2 + 18^2 = C^2$$
$$144 \text{ inches} + 324 \text{ inches} = 468 \text{ inches}$$

The square root of 468 inches is 21.63 inches, which is 1.80 feet, or 1 foot 9⅝ inches.

The gable end of a roof may also need an overhang to match the eaves overhang. You can create a slight overhang without adding extra rafters. You simply add blocking to the side wall, and add a trim board, often called a rake board. To build a deeper overhang, you can add fly rafters.

SMART TIP   4

The Pythagorean Theorem used to figure rafter length is the same theory behind the 3-4-5 method to determine if corners are square.

Building Practices

RAFTER CUTS

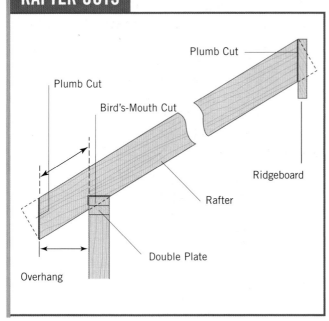

Plumb Cut

Plumb Cut

Bird's-Mouth Cut

Ridgeboard

Rafter

Double Plate

Overhang

GABLE RAFTER LAYOUT

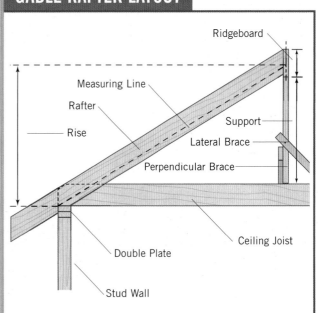

Ridgeboard

Measuring Line

Rafter

Rise

Support

Lateral Brace

Perpendicular Brace

Double Plate

Ceiling Joist

Stud Wall

FRAMING A GABLE ROOF

After you lay out and cut the first rafter, use it as a template to lay out the second one. You can test the two rafters for fit on the ground by placing the bird's mouths over each end of a 2×4 you have cut to a length equal to the width of the building measured across the top plate. But it's best to test the rafter against the ridgeboard. If you're installing ceiling joists, nail these in place before erecting the rafters. This also stiffens the side walls against push-out as you install rafters and provides a working platform.

Cutting the Ridgeboard. Cut the ridgeboard to length, and mark the rafter positions on it and on the top plates. If the roof will overhang at the gable ends, allow for the overhang at each end when you cut the ridgeboard. In many cases, it pays to let the ridgeboard run long and trim it to exact length after the last rafters are installed and the layout is checked.

Preassembling End Rafters. On small sheds you may be able to assemble some components on the ground. For example, you might attach two end rafters to the ridgeboard, adjust the spread of the rafters, and nail a temporary cleat to hold them in position securely as you raise the assembly into place. In most cases, you need to fix the ridgeboard in its final position ahead of time and brace it very securely so that it doesn't move as you nail up rafters one at a time.

Adding the Remaining Rafters. Once the end rafters are nailed in place, you can add the remaining rafters. On most projects, you can face-nail through the ridge to set the first rafter only. You have to toe-nail the second rafter. Codes may require hangers.

Adding Strapping. Before you add any other framing, be sure that the rafter layout is correct. On all but small sheds, you should add strapping perpendicular to the rafters at midspan to keep the rafters square and prevent bowing.

Framing the Gable End. Now you can add studs along the gable-end walls. Each one gets two cuts to make a lap onto the rafter. The depth of the cut is equal to the thickness of the rafter so that the stud face is flush with the rafter face. The base cut in the lap has to be angled to match the angle of the rafter. At the bottom, toenail the

STEPPING OFF RAFTER LENGTH	
TOOLS	**MATERIALS**
Framing square with stops	Rafter (to serve as a template)
Combination square	
Pencil	

1 Before marking a rafter, sight down its length to see which side is crowned or raised. Install all the rafters with the crowns facing up.

2 Pivot the square until the edge of the stock near you aligns with the unit rise mark on the tongue and the unit run mark on the blade.

3 Step along the rafter, laying out in 12-in. units of run. When the layout reaches the ridgeboard, deduct half its width from the rafter length.

INSTALLING THE RIDGEBOARD & RAFTERS

TOOLS
Circular saw and handsaw
T-bevel square and framing square
4-ft. level
C-clamps and hammer
Measuring tape, pencil, and safety goggles

MATERIALS
Two-by ridgeboards
2x4 post
2x4 bracing
Common nails

base to the top plate of the first floor wall. At the top, nail through the rafter into the lapped portion of the stud.

Attaching Collar Ties. Some roof designs also require collar ties. These short horizontal timbers turn the inverted V-shape of rafters into an A-shape. Collar ties hold opposite rafters so that they can't spread apart.

1 For maximum safety, build a plumb post with a cleat extension to temporarily support the ridgeboard. Tack or clamp two braces at right angles; check the post for plumb; and nail the braces.

2 Set the ridgeboard on the brace post, leaning it temporarily on the 2x4 cleat. Then clamp it in position. A few screws will also work.

3 You can use the supported and braced ridgeboard as a guide to mark the correct plumb-cut angle on your rafters. Use a sliding T-bevel to mark the rafter cut; then cut it using a circular saw.

MARKING RAFTER CUTS

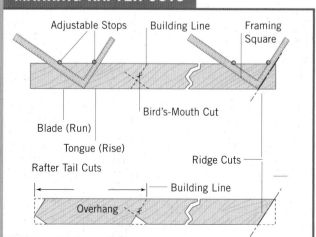

Adjustable Stops   Building Line   Framing Square

Bird's-Mouth Cut

Blade (Run)

Tongue (Rise)

Rafter Tail Cuts

Ridge Cuts

Building Line

Overhang

To mark plumb rafter cuts, such as the ridge cut and tail cut, set a framing square on the rafter with the blade and tongue measurements set at the rise and run of your roof.

FRAMING THE GABLE END

Use a plumb bob to find the center of the gable-end plate under the ridgeboard. For vents, measure one-half its width to each side of center and mark for the first full studs. Continue to mark along the plate at your stud spacing. Set a stud at a full stud position; plumb it; and mark where it intersects the end rafter. Set the stud at the next stud position, and mark it again. The difference in height is the common difference between studs. Cut notches 5 to 6 inches long and 1½ inches deep into the tops of several studs, matching the bottom of the notch to the rafter angle. Cut the studs to fit between the top plate and the end rafters, using the difference determined earlier. Toenail the studs to the plate, and nail through the rafters using 16d nails.

Vent Frame

Notched Studs

Rafter

Side Wall

Top Plate

Gable-End Stud Wall

INSTALLING GABLE-END OVERHANG RAFTERS

Aside from a hip roof, which allows for an overhang on all four sides, most roofs provide only two overhangs. If you want to match the eaves overhang at the gable ends, for example, you need to add a set of boards, called barge rafters or fly rafters next to the last common rafter.

There are two ways to attach them. As a general rule, for overhangs 12 inches wide or less, you can build a rake ladder made of two identical rafters attached to each other with two-by blocking. The inner side of the ladder is face-nailed to the end rafter, and the outer side is stabilized by nailing it to the extended ridgeboard. This system works best for roofs finished with relatively lightweight material, such as asphalt shingles.

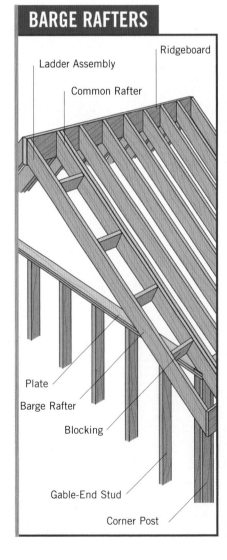

BARGE RAFTERS

Ladder Assembly

Ridgeboard

Common Rafter

Plate

Barge Rafter

Blocking

Gable-End Stud

Corner Post

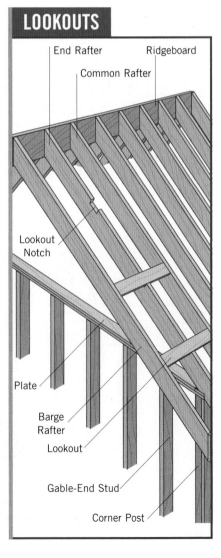

LOOKOUTS

End Rafter

Ridgeboard

Common Rafter

Lookout Notch

Plate

Barge Rafter

Lookout

Gable-End Stud

Corner Post

The other method involves notching out the end rafter for lookouts. In some cases these boards sit on edge like rafters, but extend out past the gable-end wall at right angles to the main rafters. They provide extra support and needed nailing bases for roof sheathing and roofing materials. Another option is to recess lookouts on the flat into the end rafter and butt one end into a common rafter and the other into the barge rafter.

FINISHING THE OVERHANG

The eaves section of the roof generally is called the overhang, or cornice. There are a number of different ways to finish the area. You can take the simple approach and leave the overhang open for ventilation. The roof sheathing is left exposed between the rafter tails, and the siding stops below the rafters. You can add a fascia—a long board that covers the ends of the rafter tails. This addition is wise on overhangs of more than a few inches because it keeps the rafter tails square, and provides a support surface for gutters, among other things.

Overhangs can also be soffited or boxed. In these types of designs, horizontal siding material or sheets of plywood (usually with some kind of ventilation added) is fastened in place between the fascia and the wall.

INSTALLING THE FASCIA

Before installing a fascia, snap a chalk line across the ends of the rafter tails, and check the end of each with a framing square (for square-cut ends) or a level (for plumb-cut ends). Trim any rafter tails that are not even.

The simplest fascia is a continuous piece of two-by lumber. The fascia can be even with the top of the rafter, or be trimmed with a bevel cut along the top as a finish detail.

OVERHANGS

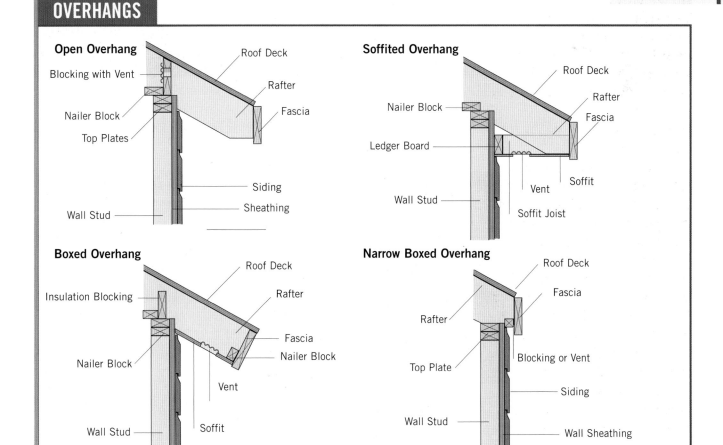

Open Overhang
Blocking with Vent
Nailer Block
Top Plates
Wall Stud
Roof Deck
Rafter
Fascia
Siding
Sheathing

Soffited Overhang
Nailer Block
Ledger Board
Wall Stud
Roof Deck
Rafter
Fascia
Soffit
Vent
Soffit Joist

Boxed Overhang
Insulation Blocking
Nailer Block
Wall Stud
Roof Deck
Rafter
Fascia
Nailer Block
Vent
Soffit

Narrow Boxed Overhang
Rafter
Top Plate
Wall Stud
Roof Deck
Fascia
Blocking or Vent
Siding
Wall Sheathing

This extra step creates continuous support for the roof sheathing. Some people prefer to install two-by lumber, called a subfascia, and finish its face with a one-by fascia that matches the trim on the rest of the building.

MARKING & CUTTING SHED RAFTERS

TOOLS	MATERIALS
Framing square and measuring tape	Rafter lumber
Circular saw	12d nails or 2-in.galvanized deck screws
Hammer or drill-driver with screwdriver bit	

1 To mark the bird's-mouth cuts on the lower wall, have a helper hold the rafter at the roof peak. Typically, the cut will be at least 1½ in. deep. Outline the position of the cap plates with a pencil.

3 Test-fit the shed rafter against the high- and low-wall top plates. If the rafter fits, use it as a template to mark and cut the rest. Then toenail the rafters at their on-center locations on the plates over the studs below.

SOFFITED & BOXED OVERHANGS

A boxed cornice generally is blocked out slightly from the wall and doesn't use soffit joists. This detail is more than adequate on basic sheds where you want the look of an overhang or the chance to provide a narrow strip of ventilation.

A soffited cornice has additional framing that connects the facia to the shed wall. The framing creates a flat area, called a soffit, that generally is covered with plywood. Most soffits include vents to allow air to sweep up into the roof along the entire overhang on both sides of the building. You can use plug vents between rafters, strip-grill vents that extend along the overhang, or perforated panels instead of solid sheets of plywood.

2 Remove the rafter, and use a circular saw to make a bird's-mouth cut at the marks. Don't overcut the marks; this will weaken the rafter. Instead, finish the cut with a handsaw to make the notch area drop out.

SHED RAFTER CUTS

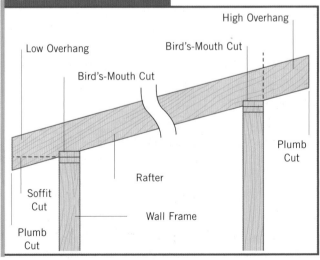

Shed Roofs

Shed roofs are like one half of a gable roof. They are easy to design and build because they have only one shallow slope with basic rafters that notch over the low wall and the high wall in a straight run. Before cutting, be sure to sight each rafter, and make sure the crown edge is facing up.

If you're framing the building walls with 2×4s, the bird's-mouth seat cuts on the rafters should be 3½ inches wide. Using the framing square, line up the blade with the building line and move the square up or down until the 3½-inch mark on the tongue intersects the underside edge of the rafter. Draw the 3½ -inch-long seat-cut line.

The bird's-mouth plumb-cut line runs from where the seat-cut line intersects the building line (inside line for the top of the rafter and outside line for the bottom of the rafter) down to the rafter edge. The depth of the bird's-mouth plumb cut should not exceed one-third the width of the rafter.

Roof Trusses

If you're nervous about cutting rafters from scratch and you don't mind losing the open attic space, roof trusses are a good option. On small sheds, trusses are usually 2×4s held together by gussets, which are flat metal or plywood plates that cover and reinforce the joints. The two top chords and one long bottom chord form the shape of a gable roof. Internal framing members, called webs, tie the chords together. Cutting any one of the members compromises the structural integrity of the entire truss.

Roof trusses commonly come in two forms, the Fink and Howe truss. But there are many different configurations and sizes. End trusses often don't have the same webs as the trusses for the interior of the roof. Instead, the webs are vertical two-by studs installed at 16 or 24 inches on center.

Order trusses from a truss manufacturer by specifying the length of the bottom chord, which should include the span, wall thicknesses, and soffits. Trusses tend to come in low-angle pitches.

SETTING TRUSSES

Lightweight 2×4 trusses for a small shed are easy to set up. The key is to add braces and strapping to trusses as you set them in position. But the only way to erect large trusses is with a crane, which is an expensive and potentially hazardous proposition best left to a professional.

The First Truss. Before lifting up the first truss, nail short two-by boards on the gable ends of the structure to act as stops so that the truss doesn't slip off the end of the plate. These can be removed when the sheathing is in place.

The best approach is to set the truss upside down, hanging from the wall plates peak down. Then walk it into place and turn it upright after calculating where the bottom chord will land on the plate. You need to work carefully.

Bracing the First Truss. Positioning the first truss is relatively easy on a small shed. It's more time consuming to brace it securely. You'll need several long 2×4s that reach down to the ground, and lateral braces that pin the truss in place on the gable-end wall. Because the rest of the trusses will depend on the stability of this first truss, you should include at least two braces running from the truss down to cleats on the floor.

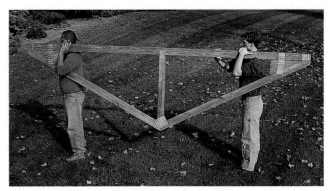

Trusses for small buildings, such as this 12-ft. truss for a 4-in-12 gable-roofed barn, can easily be carried and raised into position by two strong people.

Adding Strapping. With strapping passed up from below, tie trusses together with at least one line of strapping on each side of the ridge. Use a strong material, such as 2×4 boards or ¾ furring. You can stagger the strapping temporarily and use short boards in a pinch to secure the next truss in line. Another option is to leave some strapping extended into the next bay before you tip up the truss. But after several trusses are installed, you should go back to the end wall, double check for plumb, and install a continuous strip of strapping on each side of the ridge.

ERECTING TRUSSES

TOOLS	MATERIALS
Hammer	Trusses
Stepladders or scaffolding	16d nails
4-ft. spirit level	2x4s for braces, blocking & strapping
Measuring tape	

The Last Truss. Setting the last few trusses in place can be difficult if you do not have a crane because there isn't much room to maneuver them. You often have to raise them peak up. Set the last truss against two-by stops on the gable-end plate to keep it from slipping off during positioning. Check all trusses for plumb. Attach trusses to the top plate using 16d nails.

1 Place the first truss on one end of the building and its ends on the cap plate with the top pointing downward. Two or more people will be needed to raise it upright depending on its size.

2 Fasten the truss to the cap plate using 16d nails or metal anchor brackets. Plumb the truss with a level, and nail it off to 2x4s braces that run to the ground.

3 Mark the positions of all the trusses on the cap plates. Nailing 2x4 spacer blocks between the truss locations will stabilize a truss while it is toenailed into place.

4 Set the second truss in place against its spacer, and toenail it to the cap plate with four 16d nails or fasteners specified by the truss manufacturer.

5 With three trusses installed, tack strapping across the top on each side. Nail strapping on additional trusses as you set them in position to tie the trusses together.

BASIC TRUSS TYPES

Howe

Fink

Pratt

King Post

Queen Post

Gable End

Howe Scissors

Gambrel

Mono

Mansard

Gambrel Roofs

Gambrel roofs are often found on barns and utility buildings because the design allows for more usable room on the topmost floor. Remember that you need to take this area into account when you plan the building. Adding second-floor joists suitable for heavy-duty storage can increase the load on exterior walls and foundations.

Basic Gambrel Design.

A gambrel roof is really a combination of two gable roofs with varying slopes. The part of the gambrel roof that rises directly off the top plates—the first gable—tends to have a severe slope, such as 16 in 12, which is a ⅔ pitch. The part of the gambrel roof that rises to the ridge—the second gable roof— has a less severe slope—often something like 8 in 12, which is a ⅓ pitch. With stick framing, you need a support such as a wall or a horizontal beam, possibly with posts, wherever the rafters on one slope meet the rafters on another. These cuts and joints can be tricky. In a true gambrel roof, the two parts of each side of the roof have rafters of the same length, and all four rafters describe chords of a semicircle. (See "Gambrel Truss Layout," page 88) Not all gambrel-style designs fit this pattern, however. A common layout—easier to calculate and measure—has the upper and lower roof angles at 30 and 60 degrees respectively. (See this type on the left at the top of the next page.)

MEASURING FOR A GAMBREL ROOF

For measuring purposes, a gambrel roof is divided into two different roofs with two different rises and runs. The total run for the lower part of the gambrel roof is found by measuring the distance from the cap plate of the building wall to the center of the cap plate of a mid-pitch

SMART TIP **4**

Building Practices

When accepting delivery of roof trusses, make sure the truck gets as close to your building site as possible. Some dealers will provide a crane to lift the trusses into place for a fee.

supporting wall. The total rise is the distance the roof section rises from the floor to the top of the wall. The total run for the top part of the gambrel roof is found by measuring from the cap plate of the mid-span supporting wall to the center of the ridgeboard. The total upper-portion rise is the vertical distance from the support wall's cap plate to the center of the ridge.

It's important to plan for the wall or other support system where the two slopes meet, unless you use a code-approved truss design that does not require additional support.

You can build standard gambrel rafters that join over the double plate of a support wall, buy gambrel roof trusses, or, for a small-scale project, build your own trusses on-site.

GAMBREL TRUSS LAYOUT

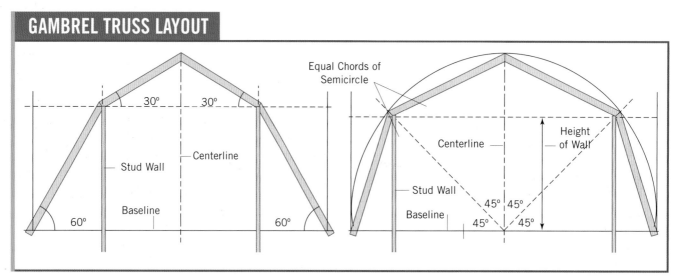

A simple layout for a gambrel roof has the first set of rafters at a 60° angle to the baseline and the second set of rafters at a 30° angle. In gambrel designs you need to support the joint at rafter segments with a beam (like a low-set ridgeboard) or a bearing wall.

A true gambrel roof—one that will give you more space in the second story—has rafters of equal lengths that describe chords of an imaginary semicircle. The intersections of the rafters and the peak of the roof will be the same distance from a central point.

PREFABRICATED GAMBREL TRUSS

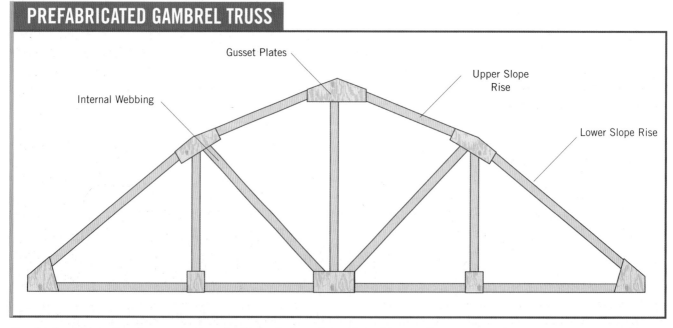

Gambrel roofs are the shape many people think of when they think of barns. They consist of two different sets of rafters or different slopes, often joined together by a plywood or metal gusset plate.

MARKING & CUTTING GAMBREL TRUSSES

TOOLS

Chalk-line box
Pencil
Sliding T-bevel
Circular saw
Power drill with screwdriver bit

MATERIALS

Two-by lumber for rafters and chord
1½-in. screws
Plywood for gussets

1 Obtain the roof slope and run from the plans, and then determine the rise. Snap chalk lines on a concrete slab (or driveway) marking the roof outline, including an overhang at the eaves.

2 Estimate the length you will need for each of the four rafters in the truss, leaving a few inches extra. Lay them down with the horizontal bottom chord over your chalk lines.

3 Mark the cut lines onto the rafters with a sliding T-bevel. The two cuts should align with the radius line that intersects with the center of the layout. Cut the marks with a circular saw.

MAKING GAMBREL TRUSSES

The easiest approach is to build trusses on the deck or slab before framing the walls. You need a flat surface to make an accurate assembly.

One option is to make what amounts to a full-scale drawing of the truss on the slab using a chalk-line box. Start by snapping a baseline across the short dimension of the floor so that you won't run into the anchor bolts that are sticking out of the concrete. Find the center of your baseline, and snap a perpendicular line. Measure and mark a point above the baseline to define the peak. Then snap diagonals running from the peak to each end of the baseline as if you were defining the bottom edge of two gable rafters.

Next, snap a mid-line that runs above and parallel with the baseline, and two lines running from the midpoint of the baseline through the intersections with the diagonals. There are no hard rules governing the offset of the two gambrel roof planes. (For two popular approaches see, "Gambrel Truss Layout," opposite page.) Once the offset points are established, snap the bottom edges of the gambrel lines, running the chalk line from the peak to the offset point and from the offset point to the end of the baseline on both sides.

SMART TIP 4

Check gambrel truss plans with your local inspector. Very small spans may be allowable with gusset plates only. However, due to the weak link at each two-part rafter, you may need internal webs.

4 Lay the rafters back on the chalk-line layout to make sure they fit. If they do, trace a plywood gusset to fasten them together. Attach gussets using 1½-in. screws. Cut the gusset flush with the top of the rafter.

Wall Sheathing

With the exterior walls plumb, square, and braced, it's time to add sheathing. You can apply sheathing vertically or horizontally. Horizontal sheathing is generally a better choice, although some building codes require that you put 2×4 blocking behind the horizontal seams.

Vertical sheathing is a good choice on 8-foot-high walls where you have a nailing surface along all four edges of the plywood. But on walls where the inside height is 8 feet, the outside wall may be higher, and you will need to extend sheathing over ceiling joists (if there are any).

If you sheathed these walls vertically, you would need to fill in strips at the top. That could compromise the superb racking resistance of plywood or oriented-strand board. Installing fill strips between full horizontal sheathing panels in the middle of the wall is a better approach and maintains better racking resistance.

Also, most wall designs call for the bottom edge of sheathing to overlap the sill plate and cover some of the foundation or slab. This overlap provides the wall with shear resistance and helps to seal out drafts and insects.

When sheathing walls, it's often easiest to sheath right over the rough openings that you created within your stud framing. When you're finished sheathing, you can mark the openings from the inside and cut them out from the outside with a reciprocating saw or a circular saw.

MATERIAL CHOICES

Many types of sheathing materials are available—from gypsum and fiberboard nonstructural sheathing to oriented-strand board and conventional plywood—all in a variety of thicknesses. Your plans will probably specify the kind of sheathing to use. One-half-inch CDX plywood rated for use on exterior walls is the most common type of material for outbuildings that are sheathed.

INSTALLING SHEATHING

TOOLS	MATERIALS
Measuring tape	Sheathing material (plywood or OSB)
Hammer or drill-driver	
Screwdriver bit	6d or 8d common nails or 1½-in. screws
Chalk-line box	
Circular saw	2x4s for blocking (if required by code)
Handsaw or reciprocating saw	

1 The edges of sheathing should fall over studs. Use a chalk line to mark stud locations.

2 Screw or nail the sheathing every 6 in. along the edge and every 12 in. in the interior.

3 In horizontal applications, if two sheathing panels don't reach the top of the wall, you'll need a filler strip of plywood installed between the two.

4 For each rough opening, drive a nail or drill small holes from inside through the sheathing at the four corners.

5 Cut the rough openings using a circular saw. Plunge-cut into the sheathing, and continue cutting to the corners of the box.

SHEATHING THE ROOF

TOOLS	MATERIALS
Hammer	Plywood sheathing
Measuring tape	8d nails or power stapler
Circular saw	Panel clips (for 24-in.-on-center framing)
Chalk-line box	Drip edge
Sawhorses	15-pound asphalt-impregnated roofing felt
	⅞-in. roofing nails

Roof Sheathing

Most shed roofs require ½-inch-thick plywood or other panel material rated for exterior use. When you install sheathing over rafters, stagger the end joints so that the seams don't line up. If you start with a full 4x8 sheet along the eaves, use a half sheet to start the next course. Prolonged exposure to the weather can damage the framing, so waterproof the roof sheathing as soon as possible.

Plan any panel cutting so that you can use the cutoff portions on the opposite side. You can start at the eaves with a full 4-foot-wide panel, provided you don't end up at the top having to use a strip less than 16 inches wide. A narrow strip may be too weak to support a person or provide a solid backing for the roofing. Trim the panels of the first row as needed to adjust the width of the last row. Also plan to stagger panels in succeeding rows so that the ends fall on different framing members.

Cover the sheathing with roofing felt before applying th finished roofing. In temperate climates, apply one layer of 15-pound felt on roofs having a 4-in-12 or greater slope. Lap the felt at least 2 inches horizontally and 6 inches vertically to shed water. Overlap the ridge by at least 6 inches. On roofs having less than a 4-in-12 slope, start with a 19-inch-wide sheet along the eaves. Lay a 36-inch-wide sheet over that, and then lap each subsequent sheet 19 inches horizontally and at least 12 inches vertically.

Use caution working on the roof at all times. Remember, the greater the roof slope, the more hazardous the job.

1 If fascia will be nailed to the rafter tails, the edge of the bottom course of sheathing should not protrude past the rafter's tail cut.

2 Begin at a bottom corner, placing the long side perpendicular to the rafters. Use 8d nails every 6 in. along the edge and 12 in. in the field.

3 To support the panel seams where they fall between rafters, use plywood panel clips.

4 Start the second course with a half panel to stagger the joints.

SMART TIP 4

On steep roofs, attach 2x4 cleats to the sheathing for footing support.

Building Practices

Adding Electrical Power

Providing your shed with electrical power will give you the opportunity to install lights and electrical receptacles. The way you plan on using the shed will determine the power requirements, but for most garden sheds, plan on adding a dedicated circuit to the house's existing panel box.

To run electrical power from the main house to your shed, use underground feeder and branch-circuit cable, known as UF cable. It is designated for outdoor wiring because it is weatherproof and suitable for direct burial. The wires are molded into plastic rather than wrapped in paper and then sheathed in plastic as NM cable wires are. Aboveground UF cable must be protected with conduit where subject to damage.

Direct-burial cable must be buried deeply enough to be protected from routine digging. The National Electrical Code specifies minimum depth requirements for underground cable: 24 inches for direct-burial cable; 18 inches for rigid nonmetallic conduit; and 6 inches for rigid and intermediate metal conduit.

If your cable is protected by a GFCI, you may be permitted to trench less deeply, but this is not recommended—you might someday plant a tree or shrub over the cable and risk cutting it while digging.

Any special characteristics of newer types of

RUNNING CABLE FROM THE HOUSE	
TOOLS	**MATERIALS**
Insulated screwdrivers	12-3 or 12-2 with ground NM cable
Measuring tape	Mounting bracket
Needle-nose pliers	Rigid conduit and pipe straps
Caulking gun	Masonry anchors
Sledgehammer	Cable clamps and staples
Electrician's hammer	Junction box
Power drill-driver with spade or masonry bit	LB fitting
Star drill	Conduit sweep bend
Knockout punch	Conduit nipple

1 Mount the junction box over the access opening with screws, and run the branch-circuit cable from the breaker box through the hole on the side of the box.

3 A conduit sweep bend is attached below the first length of conduit. It safeguards the cable as it goes underground. A bushing at the end prevents the cable from chafing.

4 Feed exterior UF cable from the shed up the sweep bend, through the conduit and LB fitting, to the junction box inside. If you need to run conduit through the entire trench, you can do it now.

cable insulation will be identified on the sheathing, such as sunlight and corrosion resistance.

OUTDOOR ELECTRICAL BOXES

There are two main types of outdoor boxes, raintight and watertight. Raintight boxes typically have spring-loaded, self-closing covers, but they are not waterproof. This type of box has a gasket seal and is rated for wet locations as long as the cover is kept closed. It is best to mount a raintight box where it is not subject to water accumulation or flooding. Watertight boxes, on the other hand, are sealed with a waterproof gasket and can withstand a soaking rain or saturation. These boxes are rated for wet locations.

2 On the outside, use a short length of conduit, called a conduit nipple, to make a connection between the LB fitting and junction box. Turn the long end of the LB fitting down toward the ground.

5 Splice the NM cable and exterior UF cable inside the interior junction box, or you can continue the run of cable because UF cable can be used indoors as well.

CONDUIT, CONNECTORS & FITTINGS

Outdoor wiring is typically protected by rigid conduit—both aboveground and wherever it enters or emerges from underground trenching. Rigid and intermediate metallic conduit (IMC) are most commonly used, but many local codes permit the use of rigid nonmetallic conduit, which is made of polyvinyl chloride (PVC). Regardless of which type of rigid conduit you are permitted to use, you will have to make a variety of connections. These are available for metal and nonmetallic conduit, including bushings for straight pieces and elbow connections, locknuts, offsets, and various couplings. Be sure that the connectors you

SMART TIP   **4**

To add lights and an extra electrical receptacle to your shed, a 15 or 20-amp circuit should be sufficient. But to use the shed as a workshop, plan on adding more power.

Building Practices

BURIED CABLE

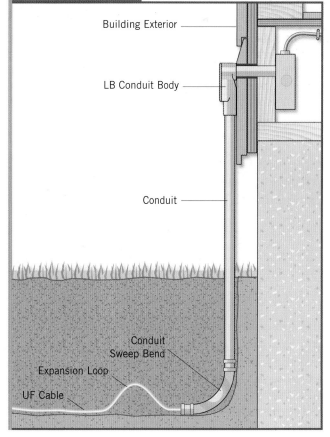

Building Exterior

LB Conduit Body

Conduit

Conduit Sweep Bend

Expansion Loop

UF Cable

RUNNING CABLE IN NEW CONSTRUCTION

TOOLS
Basic carpentry tools
Chalk-line box
Circular saw
Handsaw or reciprocating saw

MATERIALS
Sheathing material
6d or 8d common nails

1 Use a measuring tape and a pencil to measure and mark the height where utility boxes will be situated; generally this is 12 in. off the floor for receptacles and 44 in. for switches.

2 Nail utility boxes in place on the stud. Set the box out from the stud to account for the thickness of the drywall. Be sure that the boxes will be flush with the finished wall surface.

3 Using a power drill with a spade bit, drill holes through wall studs at the same height to run the electrical cable through. Drill in the center of the stud to avoid compromising its strength.

4 For vertical runs, attach the cable to the side of the stud using staples designed for use with the cable. These staples are attached by hammering them into the stud, over the cable.

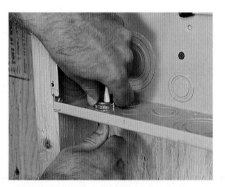

5 Where the cable passes into a device box, use a clamp connector. This not only protects the cable from chafing, it clamps it in place so that it can't be easily pulled out.

6 To run the cable horizontally, fish it through the studs, one at a time, using the holes you have drilled with a spade bit. Avoid kinking the cable or tearing the insulation.

7 Pull the cable up into the device boxes you have mounted. Be sure to pull an ample amount through, as the cable access ports on device boxes act as traps, making it hard to retract.

8 After connecting the proper wires to the proper terminals, mount switches or receptacles securely to the device box. A tight physical connection is essential for safety.

INSTALLING A FLOODLIGHT

TOOLS	MATERIALS
Screwdriver	Floodlight
Power drill-driver	Weatherproof fixture box
with screwdriver bit	Wire connectors and cable
Caulking gun	Staples and screws
	Caulk

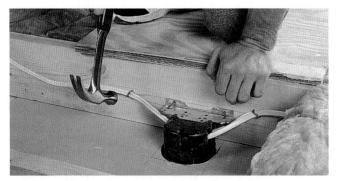

1 Extend power from a fixture or outlet in the shed to the switch box that will house the switch that will control the floodlight. Run cable from the switch box to the fixture.

2 Most fixtures have two lamp holders that swivel to cover a large area. Many also have motion sensors and timer switches that provide security and make it easier to find your keys at night.

3 Connect wire leads from the lamps to the power leads (and ground) in the box with wire connectors. Attach cover, and caulk around the box. Add lamps.

select match the material and category of conduit you are using.

At the point where cable runs through the exterior wall of your home, you will need a special L-shaped connector called an LB conduit body. An LB encloses the joint between your indoor cable and the outdoor UF cable (UF cable is also permitted for indoor use) that runs down the side of your house and into an underground trench. LB conduit bodies are fitted with a gasket that seals the cable connection against the weather.

Another type of fitting that you may find useful is a box extension which is used to increase the volume of an existing outdoor receptacle or junction box when you need to tap into it to bring power where it is required. This is often done to avoid extensive rewiring and renovation work.

OUTSIDE LIGHTS

For outdoor lighting, either type R (reflector) or type PAR (parabolic aluminized reflector) lamps are suitable. These long-lasting lamps have a reflective interior surface that maintains a bright light and resists weathering. Although PAR lamps are not affected by inclement weather, not all type R lamps are acceptable for outdoor use; check the package labeling. To mount lamps of this kind, you must install weatherproof lamp sockets. Outdoor sockets for single-, double-, and triple-lamp installations are available. Some mounts can also accommodate a motion-sensor control switch.

You can also install 120-volt or low-voltage (12-volt) exterior accent lighting. Mount a light fixture on a post to provide general lighting or on a ground spike pointing upward to show off a beautiful part of your landscape. If you choose low-voltage lighting, then you will also need to install a voltage transformer on the exterior wall.

SMART TIP **4**

For convenience and security, install exterior lights that come equipped with motion sensors. The light will switch on as you approach the shed.

Building Practices

BUILDING THE

Sheds

5

Saltbox
Garden Shed

Saltbox Garden Shed Diagram

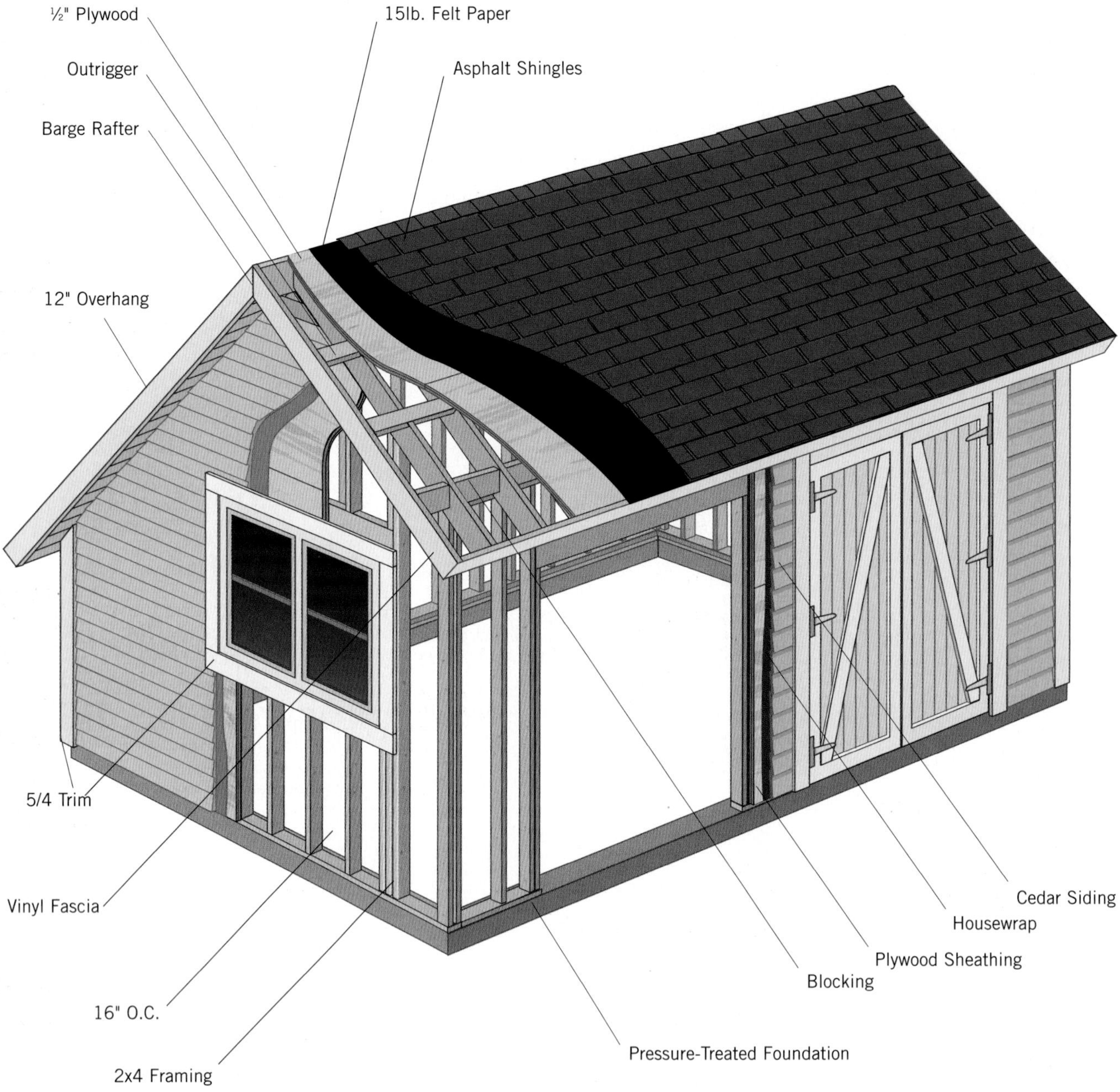

½" Plywood

Outrigger

Barge Rafter

12" Overhang

15lb. Felt Paper

Asphalt Shingles

5/4 Trim

Vinyl Fascia

16" O.C.

2x4 Framing

Pressure-Treated Foundation

Blocking

Plywood Sheathing

Housewrap

Cedar Siding

Building the Shed

If you are going to build a shed from scratch, it should not look like a prefabricated shed that you bought and had delivered, all assembled, to your site. This one differs markedly from a prefab in appearance, spaciousness, and construction. And it will last as long as your house does.

Inside the shed, you have a generous overhead space and ample floor space for a garden bench and storage shelves. And of course, it's the perfect shed for parking your lawn tractor and trailer, wheelbarrow, shredder, snowblower, string trimmer, leaf blower, and full complement of shovels, rakes, and pruners. The windows and doors let in plenty of light, so you won't lose small tools in dark corners.

Design Basics. The shed measures 12 × 16 feet, with two pairs of wide, hinged doors and windows in both end walls. The walls are framed with 2×4s, with ½-inch plywood or OSB sheathing. The siding is beveled western red cedar; the painted wood trim is ¾ pine.

The shed is built on a foundation of 6×6 pressure-treated timbers set on a gravel footing. The floor is compacted screenings, or fine gravel. The screenings can be wet down and compacted to form a smooth, hard surface. This circumvents the labor and expense of building a concrete slab.

Roofing. The height of the roof ridge presents the biggest challenge, and using scaffolding is essential. After you have framed and erected the front and back walls, set up your scaffolding in the center of the floor to install the rafters.

MATERIALS LIST

FOUNDATION

8 pcs.	6x6 16'
8 pcs.	6x6 12'
84 spikes,	10" galvanized
20 rebar spikes	18"
gravel	
screenings	

FRAMING AND SHEATHING

28 sheets ½" CDX plywood

2 pcs.	2x10	10'
19 pcs.	2x8	12'
19 pcs.	2x8	8'
3 pcs.	2x6	12'
7 pcs.	2x4	16'
5 pcs.	2x4	14'
12 pcs.	2x4	12'
28 pcs.	2x4	10'
11 pcs.	2x4	8'
4 pcs.	1x8	10' No. 2 pine

12d common nails
8d common nails

ROOFING

9 pcs. aluminum drip edge, 10' long
3 rolls, 15 lb. builder's felt (total of 296 needed for roof and walls)
13 bundles of shingles (3 bundles per square)
⅞" roofing nails
⅝" staples
2 tubes asphalt cement

WINDOWS

4 double-hung windows, 34" x 36"

TRIM BOARDS

15 pcs.	¾ x6	12' No. 2 pine
6 pcs.	¾ x6	14' No. 2 pine
6 pcs.	1x6	12' No. 2 pine
6 pcs.	1x8	10' No. 2 pine

12d finish nails
3 tubes latex caulk
1 gal. latex exterior primer
1 gal. latex exterior paint

SOFFITS AND FASCIA

13 pcs. vinyl soffit, 12' long
8 pcs. vinyl fascia, 12' long
8 pcs. vinyl J-channel
aluminum trim nails

SIDING

1060 lin. ft. ½" x 8" western red cedar beveled siding
2" aluminum siding nails
1¼" stainless-steel screws
1 gal. latex semi-transparent exterior stain

DOORS

4 shts.	¾"	exterior birch plywood
13 pcs.	1x6	8' No. 2 pine
1 pc.	1x8	8' No. 2 pine

2 tubes construction adhesive
6d finishing nails
12 T-hinges
48 screws, 3" No. 12
48 hex bolts w/washers, split washers, and nuts, ⁵⁄₁₆" x 2"
2 clasps and staples w/mounting screws
2 sliding bolts w/mounting screws

SMART TIP | **5**

Once you have outlined the base of the new shed, double-check that the location meets any setback requirements that apply.

Saltbox Garden Shed

The Foundation

The saltbox shed is built on a perimeter foundation composed of 6×6 pressure-treated timbers spiked together with 10-inch galvanized nails. It's a practical, easy-to-construct foundation that even a lone builder can complete, though it sure is nice to have some help hefting the timbers.

It's important to extend the foundation down below the frost line and to promote drainage away from the foundation. You can hire an excavator to dig the foundation trenches and strip the sod from the interior area using a backhoe. The work takes well under half a day.

Spread gravel in the trenches; then lay the first course of timbers. Naturally, the number of courses needed depends on how deep your trenches are. The goal is to have the top surface of the foundation just a few inches above grade.

Take the time to do a good job of leveling and squaring the first course. Having to compensate for a pitched, out-of-square base will make it difficult to frame a square and plumb shed.

Build the

1 Use two tape measures and the 3-4-5 methods to lay out the foundation corners. When the 16-ft. side and the 12-ft. side are laid out at right angles, the diagonal measure will be 20 ft.

4 Drive rebar pins through the first-course timbers to tie them to the ground. Drill a pilot hole completely through the timber; then hammer the 24-in.-long pin in place with a hand sledge.

5 Build up the foundation with the timbers alternating at the corners. Position all four timbers for a course, and measure the diagonals to ensure the course is square. Drill a pilot hole; then spike the new course to the one below with 10-in. galvanized nails.

Foundation

2 Mark the outside corners of the foundation trenches on the ground with fluorescent spray paint. Nothing more is needed for an excavation job this simple.

3 Shovel gravel into the trenches to promote drainage. You need a layer about 6 in. deep all around. Level the gravel's surface as much as possible before setting the first-course timbers in place.

6 Backfill the trenches as soon as you can. Shovel a layer of soil into the gap between the trench wall and the foundation; then tamp it. Backfill more and tamp again. Because the soil will settle, backfill a few inches above grade.

7 Have the screenings or fine gravel dumped directly into the foundation, if possible. As you spread and level the material, tamp it methodically, either by hand, as shown, or with a power tamper.

SMART TIP 5

Tamping the floor is essential, but boring. To speed the work along, consider renting a power tamper.

Saltbox Garden Shed

The Walls

Because of the saltbox roofline, the roof is framed after the front and back walls are up but before the side walls are framed. The side-wall studs extend from the sill to the rafters, and they are cut and fastened one at a time.

In general, you frame a wall by cutting the parts, laying them out on a flat surface, and nailing them together. You nail the sheathing to the frame while it's still lying flat, primarily because it's easier to do this way. Also, it enables you to square the wall assembly before erecting it. The sheathing will keep the wall assembly square as you heave it into place.

Choose long, straight 2×4s for the plates. Set the top plates and soleplates side by side. Mark up the plates together, but on each, mark only the locations of studs that actually abut it. Code the location according to the type of stud that goes there. For example, use an "S" for a full-length stud, a "C" for a cripple, a "T" for a trimmer.

That done, cut studs and trimmers to length, and make up your corner posts and any headers needed.

Framing. Lay the frame parts for a wall on the shed floor. Line up the studs, and arrange one plate across the bottoms, the other across the tops. Drive 16d nails through the plates into the ends of each stud.

Measure the frame, and cut pieces of ½-inch CDX plywood to size. Don't worry about openings for windows or doors; you'll cut them out after nailing the sheathing to the studs. Extend the plywood 1 inch beyond the bottom plate so that it will overlap the seam between the plate and the foundation. Leave a ⅛-inch gap between pieces, and of course, size the pieces so joints between them will occur over a stud.

Next, you must set up the wall and brace it. This job requires at least two people. First of all, the wall is heavy, and once it is upright, you will need at least one person to hold it up while the other gets the bottom aligned properly on the foundation and sets up the bracing.

Once the wall is braced, drive 16d nails through the soleplate into the foundation.

The Back Wall

1 Lay out the top and soleplates for the back wall together. Measure and mark the stud locations, and mark an "X" on the side of the line where the stud will be attached.

4 Take the diagonal measurements to ensure the frame is square. You can shift the alignment of the assembly by rapping a corner with a sledge hammer. Swing the hammer as you would a putter in golf.

2 Pile identical studs with their ends flush. Mark a cut line on the top layer of studs. As you cut through the top studs you'll kerf those underneath, marking where they are to be cut.

3 Line up the plates and studs, and drive nails through the plate into the end of each stud. Use foot pressure to align the top surfaces as you drive the nails.

5 Nail the plywood sheathing to the frame once it is square. The job is easier with the frame lying flat, and the sheathing prevents the wall from shifting out of square as you lift it into position.

6 Set up the frame, and brace it. The job requires at least two: one to hold the wall and monitor the level, the other to nail the brace to the foundation.

SMART TIP **5**

When choosing studs for the walls, set bowed, crooked, and twisted lumber aside to use as scrap material or as braces.

Saltbox Garden Shed

Build the Front Wall

1 Mark up the top and soleplates together, but on each, mark only the locations of studs that actually abut it. Code the location according to the type of stud that goes there.

2 Build up a header by face-nailing two 2x8s together, with a ½-in. plywood spacer between them. The plywood doesn't have to be a continuous piece; this is a good place to use up scraps.

5 Sheathe the wall frame after squaring it. Apply full sheets of plywood, covering up the top portion of the doorways. After the wall is sheathed, snap cut lines and cut out the doorways.

6 Raise the wall into position. It is heavy; you'll need a strong helper or two to tip it up. Once the wall is tipped up, it takes little effort to hold it upright.

3 Face-nail the trimmers to full-length studs, and make up corner posts by face-nailing studs together. You can economize by sandwiching short pieces of 2x4 between the studs to form the corner posts.

4 Lay the wall frame parts on the shed floor for assembly. One by one, line up the parts on the appropriate layout lines, and nail through the plates into the ends of the studs.

7 Install temporary bracing to hold the wall erect. Nail 2x4s to the corner posts and to scraps scabbed to the foundation, as shown. Make sure the wall is plumb.

Front Wall Frame

15¼" Top Plate Header

104"

82"

25" 64" Jack Stud Full Stud

192"

Roof Framing

The biggest challenge in building the saltbox shed is framing the roof, and there are a couple of reasons for this. Because the ridge beam is longer than any standard board, you'll have to join two pieces end to end, and you will have to make the connection about 12 feet above the sill. Finally, because the shed is saltbox style, the front rafters are different from the back rafters.

You have to deal with the ridge first. Get it up, and then you can cut and fit a front rafter and a back rafter. Use the first two rafters as patterns to lay out the remaining rafters.

Unless you have several helpers, it's easiest to splice the ridgeboard after you hoist the two sections into place atop temporary supports. But lay out the rafter locations while the ridgeboard sections are on the ground (or on sawhorses, anyway). Select straight boards and prepare two splice boards, which you'll scab across the end-to-end butt joint, once the sections are aloft. The splice should fall between rafters.

Setting up temporary supports for the ridgeboard requires some ingenuity. Because the end walls aren't framed yet, you have to stand a long stud on the foundation and attach braces at right angles to hold it erect. A similar stud must be erected and braced midway between the end supports. You don't want the supports to interfere with the rafters or the splice.

Stretch a level line across the braces, and scab a 2×4 scrap to each stud. You rest the ridge on these supports and clamp it to the stud, which should extend up past the ridge. (See page 110.) After the ridge sections are clamped to the studs, attach the splice boards.

While there are a couple of methods for laying out rafters, the best for this project is the step-off, which uses a framing square. The procedure is depicted in the drawings below. (For general guidelines for cutting and installing rafters, see "Three Methods for Calculating Rafter Length," page 74.)

Two front and two back rafters must be notched for outriggers to which the barge rafters are attached. The barge rafters form the roof overhang. The barge rafters—two front ones and two back ones—are characterized by the absence of the bird's mouth. As you install the rafters, you place the notched ones flush with the ends of the walls. The outriggers set into the notches, and you nail through the adjacent rafters into their ends. The barge rafters are nailed to the ridge and to the outriggers.

Complete the roof framing by nailing blocking between the rafters, flush with the outside of the front and back walls. You can face-nail through the rafter for one side of the blocking and toe-nail the other side of the blocking. Cut and install the collar ties. Finally, cut and nail fascia boards spanning the overhanging ends of the rafters at the front and back. The fascia is a nice design detail, and its installation helps to hold the rafters in place, adding support to the entire roof assembly.

Laying Out Front Rafters

Laying Out Back Rafters

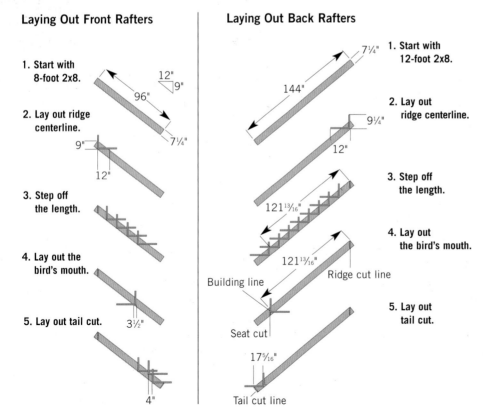

Laying Out Front Rafters:
1. Start with 8-foot 2x8.
   12" / 9"
   96"
   7¼"
2. Lay out ridge centerline.
   9"
   12"
3. Step off the length.
4. Lay out the bird's mouth.
5. Lay out tail cut.
   3½"
   4"

Laying Out Back Rafters:
1. Start with 12-foot 2x8.
   7¼"
   144"
2. Lay out ridge centerline.
   9¼"
   12"
3. Step off the length.
   121¹³⁄₁₆"
4. Lay out the bird's mouth.
   121¹³⁄₁₆"
   Ridge cut line
   Building line
   Seat cut
5. Lay out tail cut.
   17⁵⁄₁₆"
   Tail cut line

Framing the Roof

1 Mark the ridge centerline, then offset to locate the ridge cut line. Then use your framing square to step off the length of the rafter and to locate the building line.

2 Lay out the seat cut by aligning the framing square's tongue on the building line and the 4-in. mark on the blade with the rafter edge. Scribe along the blade.

3 Use the first rafter cut that fits just right as a pattern for laying out the others. Align the rafter on a 2x8 and trace the ridge cut and the bird's mouth.

4 Mark off the rafter locations on the ridge. Measure from the scarf-joint bevel on each of the two 2x8 ridge sections. Mark both sides of the ridge.

SMART TIP **5**

If you are working alone, consider buying or renting a power nailer to speed the work along.

Saltbox Garden Shed

Framing the Roof

5 Erect temporary supports for the ridge. Use chalk-line string to align the "seats" for the ridge atop the supports. Clamp the two ridge sections onto the supports.

6 The first rafter to abut the ridge at each location can be face-nailed in place. Drive three nails through the ridge into the end of the rafter.

9 Close in the spaces between rafters with blocking. Rip a bevel on a 2x8; then crosscut it into blocking. Face-nail through one rafter into the blocking, and toenail through the other.

10 With the collar tie resting on the front top plate, level it; then face-nail a collar tie to the back rafter. Then go back to the front end and face-nail the tie to the rafter and toenail it to the top plate.

7 The second rafter at each location must be toenailed to the ridge. Drive a nail through the top edge of the rafter into the ridge, and toenail through each side as well.

8 Toenail each rafter to the top plate using 16d nails. Drive nails into both faces of the rafter, angling each down into the plate.

11 For the outriggers, clamp both rafters face to face, and cut the outrigger notches in both at the same time. Remove the bulk of the waste with your circular saw. Then chisel the bottom of the notches flat.

12 Fit the outriggers into the notches, and pull their ends tight to the adjacent rafter. Drive two 16d nails through the outrigger into the rafter. Face-nail through the rafter into the end of the outrigger.

SMART TIP | **5**

Saltbox Garden Shed

When cutting notches for the outriggers or any other large notch, start the cut with a circular saw to remove the bulk of the waste. Set the blade depth so that it does not quite reach the cut line on the lumber.

Frame the End Walls

1 Setting temporary braces against the front and back walls during construction of the end walls is prudent. Nail a scrap to the wall, then butt a brace underneath it. Nail the brace to a stake in the ground.

2 One by one, stand the end-wall studs on the soleplate markings, and mark along the underside of the rafter on its edge. Use a level to ensure the stud is plumb as you mark it.

5 Plumb the stud; then drive a couple of 12d nails through the stud into the rafter.

6 Cripples are studs that extend from the soleplate to the rough sill. After the sill is set, stand the cripples one by one on the layout marks on the plate and face-nail through the sill into their ends. With the tops thus secured, it is easier to toenail the bottom ends to the plate.

3 Cut the notch with your circular saw. After making the angled shoulder cut across the stud's edge, rip in from the end to that cut.

4 Toenailing a stud to the soleplate is easy if the stud is braced against a block. Then the hammer blows won't move it off its mark.

7 The header, made up of two 2x8s and some plywood scraps, rests on trimmers that extend up from the rough sill. Set the header in place and face-nail through the full-length stud into it. Use 16d nails.

8 More cripples extend from the header to the rafters. Mark and notch these, and stand them in place. Face-nail them to the rafter; toenail them to the header.

SMART TIP **5**

When a number of window and door openings are the same size, cut the headers and sills at the same time to avoid miscutting later in the project.

Saltbox Garden Shed

Sheathe the End Walls

1 Temporarily nail a ledger to the foundation to support the ½-in. plywood sheets at the correct height. Set a sheet on the ledger; align it left and right; then nail it to the studs.

2 With the first three sheets in place, take measurements from the shed, and use them to lay out the piece of sheathing that fits the triangular gable end. The piece fits against the underside of the outriggers. The notch accommodates the ridge.

3 From inside the shed, drill a hole through the sheathing at each corner of the rough openings for the windows. Draw or snap lines from hole to hole; then saw on the lines to remove the sheathing.

Sheathe the Roof

1 The barge rafter is beyond the side wall, hanging on the ends of the outriggers. I used ⁵⁄₄ pine for this because it presented a far better appearance than any of the 2x8s that were available.

2 Nail the fascia board to the ends of the rafters. Join the fascia boards in a scarf joint, and locate the joint on the end of rafter.

3 Begin sheathing the roof at the lowest end. After the first sheets are nailed down, nail a 2x4 to the rafters to provide footing. Add additional 2x4s as you add the second row of plywood sheets, and so on up the roof. The sheets are nailed to the rafters with 8d common nails.

SMART TIP | **5**

Place sheathing material right over window and door openings. It is much easier to apply the plywood or OSB in full sheets, and then go back later to cut the openings.

Saltbox Garden Shed

Applying Roofing

A straightforward roofing job like this one requires only a tape measure, chalk line, hammer, roofer's knife, stapler for the roofing felt, and metal shears to cut the drip edge. While a pneumatic roofing nailer does speed up the work, and you can rent both the compressor and the nail gun, the saltbox shed isn't really a large job. The labor saved may not offset the cost of the rental and the time spent picking up and dropping off the equipment.

From both safety and efficiency standpoints, scaffolding is essential because you want to be able to work along the eaves from rake to rake. Roofing jacks are a worthwhile investment. Four can be spaced across the roof to support a work platform to be used when the shingle course is out of reach from the scaffolding.

Roofing the shed is not complicated. You stretch strips of roofing felt from rake to rake and staple them to the sheathing. Begin at the eave and work up the slope.

Shingling the Roof

1 Staple builder's felt to the roof. Cut the strips to span the full width of the roof. Align the first strip with the bottom edge of the roof, and staple it down. The second course should overlap the first by 4 to 6 in.

4 Lay the first full course of shingles with the tabs overlaying the starter course. Follow the nailing pattern specified by the manufacturer on the packaging. Typically, you use four nails per shingle, positioning them above the notch between tabs.

5 Begin the next several courses. The notches between tabs must be staggered from course to course, so you must cut down the first shingle in six of every seven courses. The second course begins with a 2½-tab shingle, the third with a 2-tab shingle.

2 Install drip edge to protect the edges of the sheathing. Along the lower edge of the roof, the roofing felt overlaps the drip edge. Along the gable edges, install the drip edge overlapping the felt.

3 Begin shingling the roof with a starter course. Cut the tabs off shingles. Invert the tab-free strips and position them along the roof edge.

6 As you progress up the roof, use roofing jacks to create a work platform. For each jack, drive a framing nail through the body of a shingle and into a rafter. Leave the head protruding so that you can catch the jack on the nail. Two jacks are sufficient to support an 8-ft. 2x6.

7 Remove the jacks when the roofing is complete by rolling back the tab and unhooking the jack. Seat the nail and cover the head with a dab of roofing asphalt. Roll the tab back down.

SMART TIP 5

Invert the first course of roofing shingles so that the asphalt strips are just shy of the edge of the roof. This provides sticking area for the first full course of shingles.

Saltbox Garden Shed

Install the Windows

1 Wrap the shed in builder's felt, extending the strips around the corners and across the rough openings for the windows. Each strip overlaps the one below it. Strips lap end to end, too. Staple the felt to the plywood. At the rough openings, slice through the felt with a utility knife.

2 Fold flaps of the felt over the edges of the rough window openings, and staple them to the studs, sill, and header.

3 Install the windows in the rough openings. Stand a unit on the sill and align it laterally. Then tip it up and into the opening. Make sure the nailing flange seats against the shed walls all around. Have a helper inside the shed plumb the unit with shims.

4 Drive nails through the nailing flange into the framing of the rough opening. Most windows have punched holes in the flange to indicate where to locate the nails.

Trim the Soffits and Fascia

1 Close in the eaves with vinyl soffit panels. Under the front and rear overhangs, the panels run across the rafters. Nail them to the bottom edges of the rafters. At the gable ends, fasten nailers to the side-walls parallel to the barge rafters.

2 Cut and mount short pieces of soffit to the gable end eaves. Cut the vinyl with a jigsaw or circular saw. Hook the bottom of the soffit into the interlock bead on the previously installed piece. Slide the piece along the bead to the wall.

3 Attach the soffit. Pull the piece tight, ensuring it is hooked to its neighbor; then drive aluminum or gal-vanized roofing nails through the nailing slots. A nail into the nailer and one into the rafter will hold it.

4 Cover the barge rafters and fascia boards with vinyl fascia. The lip on the fascia strip overlaps the soffit ends, and the top edge fits under the roof drip edge.

SMART TIP 5

When installing vinyl trim pieces as shown here, hold them into place using color-matched aluminum trim nails. The fasteners will be practically invisible from the ground.

Saltbox Garden Shed

The Trim Pieces

The trim applied to the saltbox shed is a significant part of its traditional design. The windows and doors are framed with wide boards, and matching boards are applied at the corners. To produce the desired appearance, use 5/4 stock for this trim. Typically 5/4 pine is 1 to 1¾₆ inches thick, and usually is stocked in standard nominal widths from 4 to 12 inches.

The trim is applied after the shed has been wrapped with felt paper or housewrap and the soffits have been trimmed out. Cut and fit the boards tight around the windows and the doorjambs. You will probably get the best fit around the windows if you cut rabbets in the trim to accommodate the nailing flange of the window. As you cut each part, tack it in place to test fit.

Before nailing the trim firmly in place, pull it down and prime the boards—front, back, ends, and edges. When the primer is dry, nail up the trim. Chalk the seam between the trim and the windows. Apply at least one finish coat to all exposed surfaces. The shed is ready for siding.

Trim the Windows,

1 Place the prefitted, preassembled, preprimed cornerboard. The board that seats against the gable-end soffit is mitered. The adjoining board is beveled at the same angle. Nail the two together, and prime them.

4 Wide, thick trim around the windows enhances their appearance. Cut and fit the parts; then prime them. If necessary, mill a rabbet into the back of each trim strip to accommodate the nailing flange so the board lies flat against the sheathing. A rabbet in the face may be needed to fit the board into the window's siding channel.

5 Set the header trim atop the windows. Align it laterally, and seat it tight against the windows. Fit the vertical trim on either side of the windows. Again, be sure it is seated tight against the window and against the header.

Doors, and Corners

2 With the corner-board assembly square against the shed walls and tight against the soffits, fasten it with 12d finishing nails. Be sure the nails penetrate the corner posts of the shed.

3 Before casing in the doorways, you must cut the soleplate out. Use a handsaw to cut flush with the studs on either side of the doorway.

6 Nail the trim to the shed with 12d finishing nails. Use a nail set to countersink the heads. Finish the installation by filling the nailholes with putty, sanding, and priming the repairs before applying a finish coat of paint.

SMART TIP **5**

Saltbox Garden Shed

Prime trim before nailing it in place. It is best to apply a coat of primer on both front and back and the edges, including the end grain. The primer acts as a sealer that helps prevent the wood from absorbing moisture.

The Siding

A lot of different siding materials are available. Beveled-wood siding is especially attractive and reasonably durable. However, the siding itself is more expensive than most other sidings, and it can be time-consuming to install. If you are building the shed yourself and you enjoy the work, time shouldn't be a major consideration, though, should it?

Western red cedar siding is used on the saltbox shed. Western red cedar is one of those woods that weathers extremely well. The siding is ½ inch (at the thicker edge) × 8 inches wide. Typically, it's delivered in random lengths, ranging in 1-foot increments from 4 feet up to 16 feet. An alternative to this siding is cedar shingles.

Cedar splits easily, so exercise care in handling and cutting it. Drill a pilot hole for every fastener you drive.

You can paint or stain cedar, and it's a good idea to apply stain or primer to the front and back before installing the siding. If you leave it natural, it will darken markedly as it weathers.

Side the Shed

1 Begin siding the shed by nailing a starter strip at the bottom of a wall. The width of the strip equals the siding overlap. Use the thin top edge of damaged siding pieces for the starter strip. Align the starter strip flush with the bottom ends of the corner boards.

4 Notching a single siding strip to fit beneath and above windows and doors is more work. Layout must be accurate, and the strip can be difficult to maneuver into position without breaking. But the payoff is a better-looking job. The alternative is to use two strips to make up the course.

2 Install the first strip of full-width siding over the starter strip. Cut it to fit tight between the cornerboards. While you might opt to use two pieces to form a single course here and there as you advance up the wall, it's best to use a single strip for the first course.

3 Cedar splinters easily. Scoring the cut line with a utility knife pays dividends—especially when the siding is prefinished—in practically eliminating the splintering. A power miter saw makes fast crosscuts, but a jigsaw is useful for notching strips as well as crosscutting them.

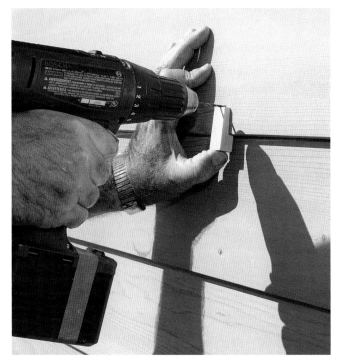

Nailing Siding

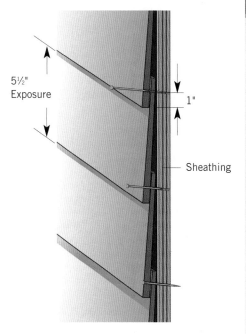

5½" Exposure

1"

Sheathing

5 Drill a pilot hole for every nail you drive through the siding. Cedar splits easily. A simple gauge aligns the bit in relation to the edge, so all the nailheads are in a line. Snap chalk lines on the builder's felt to mark stud locations.

Build and Hang the Doors

1 Build each door by attaching a wooden frame to a plywood panel. After cutting the plywood to size, use a router and V-grooving bit to cut grooves in the panel's face. Clamp a straightedge to the plywood, and guide the router along it.

2 Lay out and trim the diagonal brace for the frame before assembly. Rip and crosscut the vertical and horizontal frame members to size. Line up these parts on the plywood, and secure them with a pipe clamp at each end. Position the roughly sized diagonal brace, and clamp it.

5 Clamp the parts to one another and to the plywood while the adhesive sets. A pipe clamp applied across the vertical frame members pinches them against the ends of the horizontal parts. Bar clamps and C-clamps squeeze the parts against the face of the plywood. While the parts are clamped, drive and countersink nails.

6 Shellac any knots before priming and painting the doors. Use a dewaxed or pigmented shellac for this job. These sealers, which dry quickly, prevent the knot from bleeding through the paint. Apply a couple of coats just to the knots and pitch pockets; then prime and paint the entire door.

3 Mark the intersection of the brace and the horizontal frame piece. Set a sliding bevel to the angle as shown—the tool's body against the horizontal piece, its blade against the brace. Use this angle to scribe a cut line from the mark across the brace piece.

4 Assemble the frame to the door panel using construction adhesive and nails. The end-to-edge joints between the frame members and the brace can be aligned with biscuits. Dry assemble the parts, and clamp them. One by one, unclamp the parts, and apply construction adhesive to their backs.

7 Fit the doors, with T-hinges mounted, into the doorways, one by one, so that you can mark the hinge locations on the jambs. A permanent stop nailed to the head jamb and a temporary one tacked to the sill locate the door. Set the bottom of the door on a shim, and slide it against the side jamb.

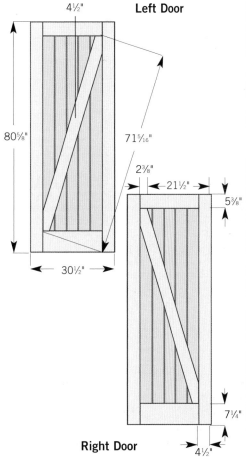

Left Door

4½"

80⅝"

71⁵⁄₁₆"

2⅜"

21½"

5⅜"

30½"

7¼"

4½"

Right Door

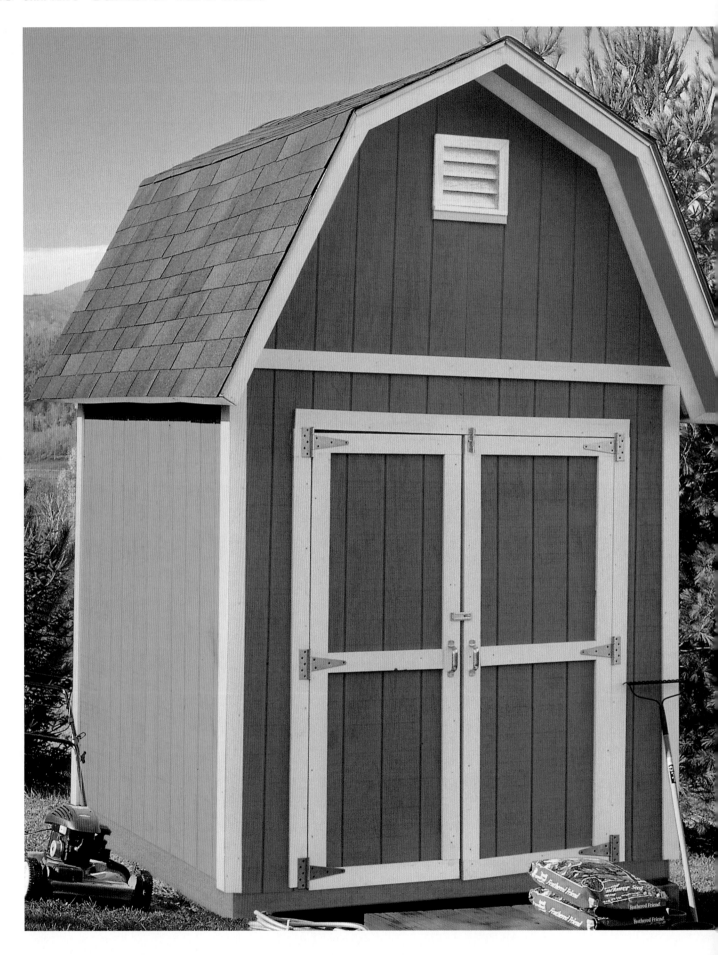

Gambrel
Yard Shed

Building the Gambrel Shed

The design shown here is a gambrel shed. It has the same walls and floors of most other buildings, but it is distinguished by its gambrel roof. A gambrel roof is really a combination of two roofs of varying pitches. In this design, the lower portion of the roof has a steep pitch, while the upper part of the roof has a pitch that is not as steep as the lower section.

Though many people prefer the crisp lines of a gable roof, a gambrel roof is ideal for a shed because it provides a great deal of storage space in the "second story" (the space created by the high-pitched rafters) even though the shed is nominally a one-story structure.

The rafters of this gambrel shed were created using site-built trusses. The bottom chords of the trusses—the 2×4s that span from wall to wall and form the bottom of the truss—create an area on which you can lay plywood to create a platform storage area, or you can use the space to hold spare lumber or items that are otherwise hard to store.

The gambrel shed shown in this chapter is 8 × 8 feet, with a substantial overhang on either end of the roof to keep water away from the siding and the foundation blocks. Using standard dimensions like these reduces the cutting of dimension lumbers and sheetgoods (plywood roof decking and siding), which come in 8-foot lengths.

Framing. The gambrel shed is framed with 2-by lumber 16 inches on center. The floor joists are made of pressure-treated wood because there is a good chance that they will come in direct contact with water from rain, runoff, and melting snow. But note that the siding is T1-11 siding, which is typically plywood. It may also be oriented-strand board, also called OSB. OSB is a patchwork of wood held in place by strong adhesive. T1-11 has grooves cut into its finished side (the side that will face outside) to give it the look of board-and-batten siding. T1-11's structural composition is similar to that of ½-inch CDX plywood, but unlike ordinary plywood sheathing, it can be painted and does not require additional finishing, as does clapboard or shingle siding.

MATERIALS LIST

FOUNDATION			
2	50-lbs bags of ¾" gravel	6 bundles	3-tab asphalt shingles
10	4" cap block	⅞" roofing nails	
12 tubes	construction adhesive		
2 pcs.	2x8 8' pressure treated	**TRIM**	
4 pcs.	2x4 8' pressure treated	20 pcs.	1x4 8' No.2 pine trim
10 pcs.	2x6 8' pressure treated		
		STAIRS	
FRAMING AND SHEATHING		4	4" cap block
11 sheets	½" CDX plywood	2 pcs.	2x8 10' pressure treated
24 pcs.	2x4 8" SPF	4 pcs.	2x6 8' pressure treated
10 sheets	4x8 T1-11 Siding		
14 pcs.	2x4 10'	**DOORS**	
2 louver vents	16" x 20"	8 pcs.	2x4 8' (for frame)
8d common nails			
12d common nails		**FINISHING**	
		6	tubes of latex caulk
ROOFING		1	gal. primer
6	4" wide drip edge (10' lengths)	2	gal. paint
1 roll	100' 10# roofing felt		

Gambrel Yard Shed

By planning your shed to be 8 or 10 feet long, you will be able to use full lengths of lumber, minimizing cutting.

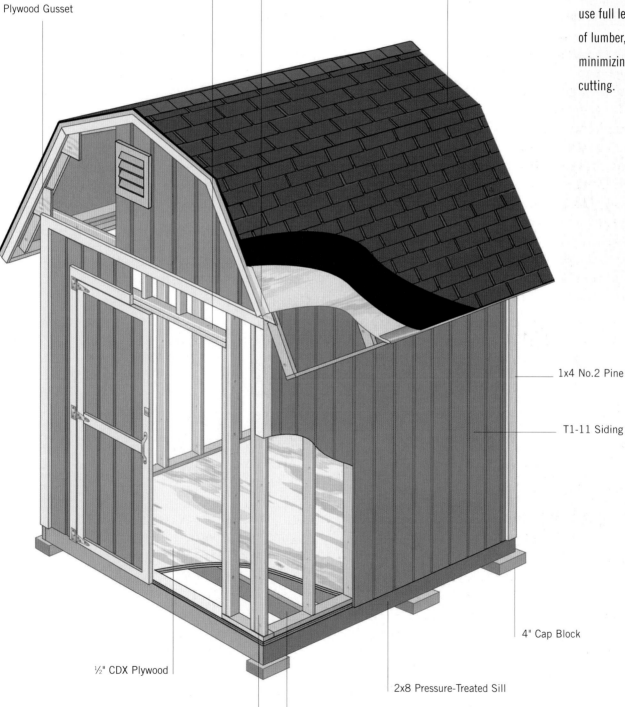

Plywood Gusset

Double Header

4" Drip Edge

Asphalt Shingles

1x4 No.2 Pine

T1-11 Siding

4" Cap Block

½" CDX Plywood

2x8 Pressure-Treated Sill

2x4 Framing

2x6 Joist 16" O. C.

The Foundation

Like the other sheds presented in this book, the gambrel shed sits on a foundation of stacked 4-inch solid concrete blocks. The blocks rest on crushed stone that goes down 8 inches. The stone base drains the area around the concrete blocks. The use of stone is also a useful tool in leveling the blocks as you can use the gravel to shim the blocks as necessary. Be sure to check with the building inspector in your area. Some codes require that sheds have a foundation that extends below the frost line.

Though the first block sits directly on the crushed stone, the remaining blocks should be glued together with standard construction adhesive, which you apply with your caulking gun. It is important that the block layout will provide you with a base to build a shed that is both level and square. Any deviation at this stage will result in your mistakes being highly visible when the building is complete. After setting the blocks, make sure that they form a square.

Framing the Floor

1 Check that the blocks create a square. Measure from the center of one block to the center of another that is diagonally across from it. If this measurement matches the other diagonal span, the base is square.

4 Once you place the 2x6 floor joists 16 in. on center, use galvanized nails to nail into the ends of the joists. Do not toenail from inside into the rim joist. You may have to shim to bring the joists flush with the rim joists.

5 Apply a bead of construction adhesive on the tops of all the rim and floor joist. This will glue the plywood in place and give the floor a firmer feel. Otherwise the floor can feel springy.

Gambrel Yard Shed

Make sure the concrete blocks are dry when you apply the adhesive. Wet blocks will not bond as well as dry blocks.

2 Once the blocks are level, set 2x8 pressure-treated rim joists in place. The 2x4 ledgers hold the joists upright while you get them level and properly positioned.

3 Because this shed is 8 x 8 feet, foundation blocks are used just in the corners, and pressure-treated 2x8 rim joists are used to form the floor frame for the shed.

6 Screw the deck in place, attaching screws every 6 in. around the perimeter and every 12 in. along the interior joists. Note that an 8 x 8-ft. floor takes exactly two sheets of plywood.

7 Snapping chalk lines over the joists will guide you for screw placement. If you do this "by eye," with no line to guide you, you may not get the screws dead center into the joists.

The Walls

The walls of this gambrel shed were framed with SPF (spruce-pine-fir) 2×4 lumber. Gang-cut the 8-foot-long studs to trim 3 inches off of each. That will allow the 8-foot sheets of T1-11 siding to extend beyond the bottom of each wall. When the wall is standing upright, the T1-11 will partially overlap the rim joist and protect it from the elements.

Because the wall is 8 feet long and the framing was done 16 inches on center, the wall is composed of exactly six symmetrical stud bays. Where possible, sheathe the walls when the stud frame is lying down, because it is easier to get the edges of the T1-11 to match exactly the edges of the 2×4s. However, it is more difficult to lift a fully sheathed wall into position. This shed is relatively small, so the average person should be able to handle the task. But even if you are able to do the job by yourself, working with at least one other person will make the job easier.

Unless you plan to finish the inside walls of the shed by applying drywall or paneling, the end studs of each wall can simply abut one another; you do not have to configure a corner to create a nailing surface for interior finishes. If you do want to finish the interior, use one of the corner framing methods described in "Stud Configurations at Corners," page 73.

Which Wall Do You Build First?

For this type of construction, it is best to build walls in opposing pairs. We started with the walls on the long dimension of the shed. Building walls in this way allows you to construct the wall on the floor of the shed, including adding the wall sheathing, and then lifting the wall into place. At this point, make sure the wall is plumb and square. Constructing the opposite wall second provides an unobstructed path to frame, sheathe, and lift the second wall into position. With two opposing end walls in place, you can add the walls that fit between them, although you may find it easier to frame these walls in place.

Building the Walls

1 Lay out stud walls on the floor deck, which can serve as a good, solid, level working surface. Mark the location of each stud on the plates ahead of time.

4 One person can easily raise an 8-ft. stud wall, but notice that a brace is in place and nailed with one nail into the side of the rim joist. This will serve to hold the wall in place once it is erected.

When working alone, determine the best positions for braces and other support systems before lifting the wall. You will save yourself a lot of time and unnecessary effort.

2 There is no need to use galvanized nails for wood framing if the nails will be covered by the roof. Nail through the top plate into the end grain of the wall studs. Use two nails per stud.

3 With the wall framed and all nailed up, lay a piece of T1-11 siding in place. Use the edges of the siding to help square up the stud wall.

5 Using a 4-ft. level, check the wall for plumb. Once it is plumb, drive a single nail through the brace into the end 2x4 on the wall. Don't drive the nail all the way home because you will remove the brace once the adjacent wall is in place.

6 With the opposing wall erected, check all walls for plumb, and then attach adjacent walls to one another. Nail through the bottom plates into the rim joist as well, using one nail per stud bay.

Making and Installing the Trusses

Trusses are a great way to frame a roof because they can be mass-produced on the ground, reduce your time on a ladder, and they bring a crisp consistency to the roofline that might be hard to attain for the beginning roof framer using stick framing. You can stick-frame the gambrel roof, as you would for a gable roof, but the geometry on a gambrel is complicated. Plus, the configuration of the truss chords, and the support each member of the truss provides, brings a natural stability to a roof truss that is hard to obtain with stick-framed rafters.

Making the Trusses. Though trusses can be ordered through your local lumberyard, they are not hard to make. Because you construct them using 2×4 lumber—not the 2×6s or 2×8s required for freestanding rafters—they are not expensive to construct. (See "Roof Trusses," page 85.)

The best way to make trusses on-site is to cut and lay out one ideal truss and assemble it on the shed floor. Once you know you have the angles right, gang-cut the remaining chords so that you can set up an assembly line to make a number of trusses at once.

For this shed, the bottom cord is 8 feet long; the rise is 4 feet. The lower cord is at a 60-degree angle to the bottom cord; the upper cord is at a 30-degree angle. This is similar to the truss layout shown on page 88. Before installing trusses, have a number of shorter 2×4s ready to act as braces. Cut a 4- and 6-foot 2×4; if you are working alone, use one long 2×4 cut at one end with a 45-degree angle to hold the first truss in place. These braces will hold the trusses up as you position them and check them for plumb.

To install the trusses, drive screws up into the bottom chord of each truss through the top plate, but you should also toenail the chords to the top plate. For extra-sturdy connections, use galvanized steel hurricane ties to attach the chords to the plates. Once the trusses are secured to the top plates and sheathed, you will have a good, sturdy roof that won't blow off in a high wind.

1 With a truss laid out on the floor deck, lay down a thick bead of construction adhesive and carefully lay the plywood gussets in place.

4 Position trusses so that they sit directly on top of the 2x4 studs. In this way, the load is carried cleanly from the roof to the foundation. Setting the first truss is the trickiest, but note that a long 2x4 cut with an angle at one end helps with the process.

Use screws rather than nails to attach truss braces. Nailing tends to knock the trusses out of plumb.

2 With the gussets positioned so that the edges are flush with the edges of the 2x4 chords, nail them in place using roofing nails. You may want to trim the gussets, to avoid sharp corners, but it's not necessary.

3 Each truss should have five gussets: one at both ends of the bottom chord; one at the peak of the truss; and one at each of the two junctures where the two roof pitches meet.

5 Each truss must be checked for plumb. As the truss is made plumb, it can be temporarily attached to the adjacent truss with 2x4 braces that will be removed later.

6 Screwing braces into place will hold the trusses until they are sheathed. The sheathing acts to stabilize the whole assembly.

Building Trusses

7 For the end trusses, it is easiest to sheath them on the ground. Lay out two sheets of siding, and place the truss on top, so you can trace your cut lines.

8 After a truss has served as a guide for drawing cut lines, use a circular saw with the blade-depth set to exactly ½ in., and cut the T1-11 siding that will be attached to the end truss.

Prefabricated Trusses

Trusses can be ordered from your local lumberyard, but stick to standard dimensions: 8, 10, 12 feet, etc., increasing in increments of 2 feet each time. You can also specify the pitch. If the trusses that the lumberyard offers aren't to your liking, you can even have custom trusses made for you, though this will be far more costly than making them on-site by yourself with 2x4 lumber. Be sure to time truss delivery for when your walls are complete. Trusses are often delivered on a "scissor truck," which acts as an elevator. The truck can lift its bed up to your roofline and slide the finished trusses right off the truck and onto the top of your walls. This can save a lot of awkward and arduous lifting.

10 For the two end trusses, sheathe them before they are erected, and then use a circular saw to create a rough opening in which to place the louver vents.

Use the first truss you make as a template for making the others. That way all of the trusses will have the same dimensions.

9 Screw the siding onto the 2x4 truss as you would attach any other sheathing, with screws every 6 in. around the perimeter chords.

11 To attach a truss firmly to a wall, screw up through the wall top plate into the bottom of the truss's bottom chord. Use at least one screw per stud bay, or at least one screw every 16 in. in open areas.

12 Screw down through the truss's bottom chord into the top plate at a diagonal. The random 2x4 braces that you see in place here will be removed once the roof is sheathed.

The Roofing

Most do-it-yourselfers can probably roof this shed in a matter of two or three hours, especially if you have a helper passing shingles up to you. Like any roof covered with asphalt shingles, this roof requires ½-inch CDX plywood sheathing and a minimum of #10 roofing felt. The 4-inch drip edge helps create a watertight seal at the edge of the plywood sheathing. (Note that in the photos shown here the 1×4 primed and painted trim was put in place along the soffit and rakes before the drip edge was installed.)

The roof on this gambrel shed has a hefty overhang all the way around the structure, keeping water away from the shed. Water is a real concern when you are using T1-11 siding; it must be kept as dry as possible. That's because T1-11 is made of plywood (or OSB), which can delaminate if it is exposed to a great deal of water. A good painted finish will also help protect the siding.

Applying Shingles. It is now widely recommended that roofers apply a course of shingles upside down all the way around the perimeter of the roof before applying the final shingles in the usual manner. This gives an extra seal where the top shingles come near the roof edge. Also note that where the pitch changes at midroof, a single course of shingles should overlap at midshingle, not at a break in courses. The shingle that spans this pitch transition will stick out for a while, and it may look rough at first, but as the sun heats the shingles, they will droop over and cover the pitch transition nicely.

Other Roofing Materials

Though asphalt shingles are inexpensive and easy to install, there are a number of other roofing products available. Let the type of roofing used on other buildings on your property and the shed's use guide your decision. The choices include cedar shakes; ag-panel, which is a ribbed metal material; and standing-seam metal roofs, which are highly durable and very attractive. Metal roofs are usually installed by professionals.

Roofing the Shed

1 Like any roof, this gambrel roof can be sheathed with ½-in. CDX plywood. Nail the sheathing every 6 in. around its perimeter and every 8 in. along the truss chords in the interior of the panel.

3 Nail 4-in. drip edge in place with galvanized roofing nails. Drip edge can be cut easily with tin snips. It gives a good, clean, crisp look to the edge of the roof, while creating a seal between the roof and the soffit-and-rake trim.

If you don't use plywood, make sure the panel you do select is rated for use as a roof sheathing.

2 The #10 roofing felt should be applied beneath the shingles before the drip edge is installed. Tack it in place with roofing nails or staples. Note that the 1x4 trim is already in place.

4 Install a course of shingles upside down—with the tabs facing in—to serve as an extra layer of protection beneath the shingles that break along the edge of the roof.

5 Three-tab shingles can be applied to any gambrel roof, just as they can be applied to a gable roof. Stagger the shingles so the seams of an upper course do not line up with the seams of the course beneath.

Front Wall and Door

The front of this gambrel shed is dominated by a large opening that will accommodate double shed doors. Although there is no need for a full-size header such as that you would find over a door in your house, the door framing should consist of both king and jack studs that are nailed together firmly. Because the doors are rather heavy—they are nearly the size of a full 4×8 sheet of ½-inch plywood—they need the double-stud support. If the hinges were attached to just one stud and the door was pulled open, the stress could loosen the hinge screws or bow the framing.

And don't skimp on the cripple studs above the door opening. They maintain the 16-inch-on-center spacing that is required for proper attachment of the wall sheathing.

Build the Door. The door of the shed is made of a 2×4 frame sheathed with T1-11 siding. There is no need for diagonal bracing because once the T1-11 is attached to the frame with glue and screws, it is substantial enough to resist racking without additional support.

In our project, we applied the sheathing to the entire wall and then carefully cut out the opening. The section removed was used for the door. This method saves money but also requires some careful cutting.

To install the door hinges, lift the door in position and mark the locations for the hinges. With the surface hinges specified here, there is no need to cut a mortise for each hinge. With two people, one can hold the door in position while the other marks the hinge locations right on the door and the front wall of the shed. Attach the hinges to the door; double-check the hinge locations on the door frame; and attach the doors.

All the trim on this shed is 1×4 No. 2 pine. It is primed on both sides to seal it against moisture. Unfortunately, No. 2 pine contains a fair number of knots, so be sure to seal the knots with a good primer or sealer, otherwise the sap from the knots will quickly bleed through the finish paint. The paint job may look fine for a brief time, but in short order you will begin to notice bleed through, especially if you use a latex paint.

Front Wall & Door

1 The rough opening for the shed doors has two studs on each side. This sturdy construction allows the shed to accommodate large swinging doors without worry that the weight of the doors will bow the framing.

4 Once the T1-11 has been cut away from the rough opening, glue and screw it to the 2x4 frame. The sheathing will prevent the frame from racking.

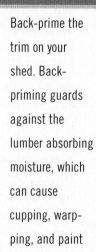

Back-prime the trim on your shed. Back-priming guards against the lumber absorbing moisture, which can cause cupping, warping, and paint failures.

2 To create the doors, sheath right over the rough opening, as though it were a normal wall, and then—with the rough opening frame as your guide—carefully cut away the sheathing that will serve as the doors. Here, the shed has already been painted. See page 142.

3 The door frame itself is made of 2x4 lumber. Because the T1-11 sheathing will be glued and screwed in place, the sheathing will provide substantial structural support for the door.

5 Once the sheathing has been attached to the 2x4 door frame, screw or nail in place 1x4 pine trim. Prime and paint the trim before attaching it to the door. It can be easily touched up once in place.

6 Install 1x4 trim to cover up any seams in the sheathing and on the corners. Trim out the shed's base and along the rake and soffits as well.

Final Touches

With the sheathing all properly nailed to prevent racking, it is time to apply the rest of the trim. Corner boards are an architectural element that bring a pleasing look to the shed. This shed has them on every corner, but not along the bottom of the long walls. By adding trim along the bottom of the sheathing, you box in the walls, creating the illusion that the shed is smaller than it really is, so avoid the bottom trim.

The luxury of T1-11 siding is that you do not have to apply another finish siding material, such as shingles or clapboard. Use a brush to paint the seams, which are really just the paths that an industrial router took to cut grooves in the siding, and then use a wide roller to apply paint to the rest of the paneling.

After the trim has been installed and the sheathing painted, it's time to build a platform, steps, or ramp up to the entry of the shed. Just as with the shed's foundation, 4-inch blocks can support a step or platform. With this finishing touch in place, the shed will have a nice finished look, with an entryway and double doors that swing wide to accommodate any activity or equipment that needs to be stored within.

Finishing

1 Using a brush, cut in the seams of the T1-11 so that the T1-11 sheathing can be easily painted with a thick roller. The raw wood is rather absorbent, so buy plenty of paint.

3 Dig pads for 4-in. solid cap blocks to serve as foundations for the steps or platform leading to the shed. The cap blocks must be level.

Building a Ramp

Though stairs or a platform are the most convenient and easy structural features to build in front of your shed, you may want to store a large piece of equipment such as a riding mower or rototiller. These items roll up ramps better than they climb stairs, so it's a good idea to have a ramp design in mind when building your shed, or at least be prepared to accommodate a removable ramp.

A temporary ramp can be made from something as simple as 2x6s laid in place when you need them. A more permanent ramp should be attached to the shed so that it does not move when in use. You may also need to build a more permanent foundation system that can take the constant movement on the ramp. The key is to be able to open the doors fully without having the swing of the doors blocked in any way. Make the ramp long enough to provide a gentle slope up to the shed.

If you plan on hanging tools or other equipment on the outside of your shed, add blocking between the studs to support the items.

2 Even though you have plumbed walls and trusses along the way, it is still important to have a 4-ft. level handy to double-check plumb on the corner boards.

4 The platform will inevitably come in contact with the ground, so assemble it using pressure-treated wood. Here 2x6s are used to create the platform on top of a 2x6 frame.

5 Once the 2x6 pressure-treated frame is assembled and set in place, check it for level. If it is not level, you can shim beneath the cap-block foundation using dirt or stone.

Gable
Potting Shed

Building the Gable Shed

The 8 × 10-foot shed profiled in this chapter is an ideal multipurpose structure, and it can serve you over the course of a lifetime. Its gable roof—with a ridgeline that rises 14 feet above the ground—allows for a roomy loft for storage (or even sleeping if the shed serves as a clubhouse). The 80 square feet of space below leaves ample room for everything from a rider mower to a mini-workshop or potting and garden-tool area.

Framing Facts. Given the standard dimensions of this structure (8 feet wide, 8 feet tall, and 10 feet long), it is simple to build with very little cutting of standard dimension lumber. When ordering materials, specify 8- and 10-foot lengths, with one 12-foot 2×8 for the ridgeboard. Using standard dimension lumber will save you a great deal of cutting during the framing stages, and it

cuts down on waste. Given that two sides of the shed are 8 feet long, framed with studs that are 16 inches on-center, you can use full sheets of plywood for sheathing. For the two 10-foot walls, 8-foot lengths of plywood will cover all but 2 feet of the wall, but you can cut a single sheet of plywood to make up the difference.

The gable roof rises 4 feet above the wall's horizontal top plates, so a single sheet of plywood, notched for the exposed ridge beam, can cover each gable end.

The foundation of this shed is simple: solid block glued together in a stack, sitting on top of gravel. In these photos, you'll see white gravel—actually marble chips. This is a purely aesthetic choice; standard ¾-inch gravel will do fine.

The 1×4 pine trim is nailed right to the underside of the soffit. With this design, you can extend the rafters beyond the walls and trim them plumb or leave them square.

MATERIALS LIST

FOUNDATION

3	50-lbs. bags ¾" gravel
18	4" cap blocks
2 pcs.	2x8 10' pressure treated
4 pcs.	2x4 10' pressure treated
10 pcs.	2x6 8' pressure treated
12 tubes	construction adhesive

FRAMING AND SHEATHING

15 sheets	½" CDX plywood
42 pcs.	2x4 8' SPF
16 pcs.	2x6 8' SPF
1 pc.	2x8 12' SPF
2 louver vents	16" x 20"
1 roll	house wrap
10d common nails	
8d common nails	
2 ½" coated screws	

ROOFING

8 pcs.	4" drip edge
1	100' roll #10 roofing felt
6 bundles	packs of 3-tab shingles
⅞" roofing nails	

TRIM AND SIDING

17 pcs.	1x4 8' No. 2 pine
10 bundles	No. 2 cedar shingles
2 ½" galvanized finishing nails	
1 gal.	cedar sealer
1 gal.	primer for trim
1 gal.	paint for trim

DOORS AND WINDOWS

1 prehung door	
2 windows	36" x 40"
1 pack cedar shims	

STAIRS

6 pcs.	4" cap block
2 pcs.	2x6 10' pressure treated
10 pcs.	2x8 8' pressure treated

Gable Shed Diagram

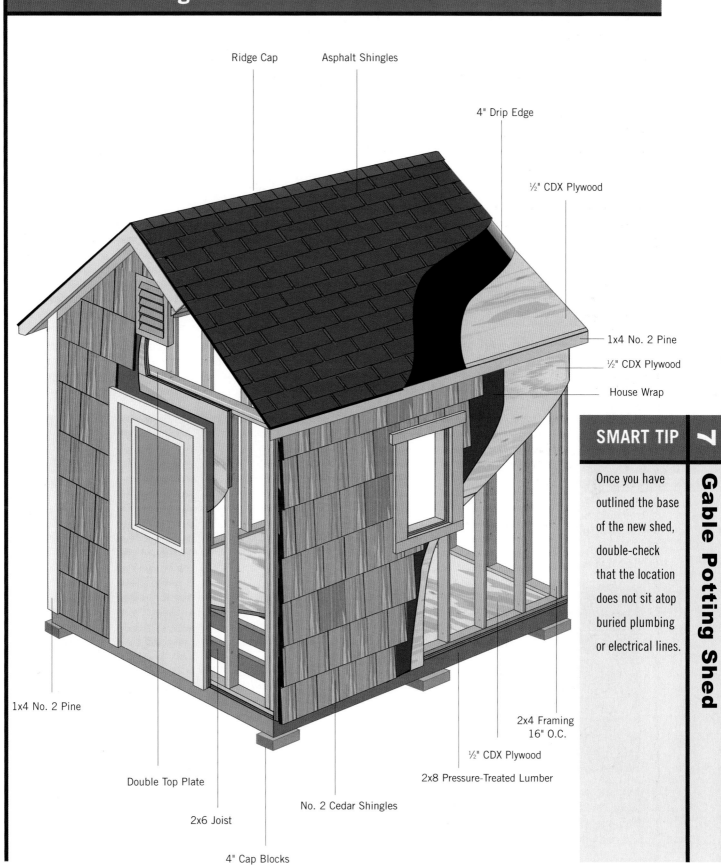

Ridge Cap

Asphalt Shingles

4" Drip Edge

½" CDX Plywood

1x4 No. 2 Pine

½" CDX Plywood

House Wrap

1x4 No. 2 Pine

Double Top Plate

2x6 Joist

4" Cap Blocks

No. 2 Cedar Shingles

½" CDX Plywood

2x8 Pressure-Treated Lumber

2x4 Framing
16" O.C.

Once you have outlined the base of the new shed, double-check that the location does not sit atop buried plumbing or electrical lines.

7

Gable Potting Shed

The Floor

Creating a straight footprint with square corners is essential. A ½-inch variation from corner to corner may not seem like much of a problem, but the discrepancy will express itself later as gaps in sheathing or a ridgeboard that isn't level.

Building on a Hilly Site

Though a good level site is desirable, it's rare to find a perfect grade for your shed. Luckily, the force exerted by the weight of a shed is a load that bears straight down, so stacked blocks can serve as a "foundation." There is no need to excavate for and pour concrete footings or walls.

When making a foundation for a hilly site, first excavate on the "high" side of the shed's footprint, and install a set of single blocks on ¾-inch gravel, dug to a depth that protects against frost heaving. (See Foundation Choices," page 52.) For the 10-foot run of this shed's rim joist (the joist that runs along the long wall), three sets of blocks will do—one at each end and one at the midpoint. For the 8-foot run, just two sets are required.

With the blocks on the high side set and level, place a 4-foot level on a straight 8-foot-long 2x4 board, and raise or lower the board until you find the approximate height of the blocks on the downhill side of your shed. Excavate pads for these downhill blocks, and fill the pads with gravel so that you achieve the desired elevation, always calculating in 4-inch, full-block increments. If the downhill blocks are an inch or two low or high, use gravel to shim beneath the blocks to raise or lower them.

Once the blocks are set and level, check the foundation for square. The corner-to-corner distance should match the corner-to-corner distance of the corresponding set of blocks.

Framing the Floor

1 With the 2x8 rim joist in place, a 2x4 ledger board provides a good bearing surface for the 2x6 joists. Using a tape measure, lay out the location for those joists so that they are 16 in. on center.

4 Glue decking to the joists, using a good thick bead of standard construction adhesive. Although the floor sheathing will be screwed in place, the adhesive gives structural stability to the shed and keeps the floor from squeaking when you walk on it.

2 Set 2x6 pressure-treated joists in place, leaving the rim joist's end grain exposed. You may need to shim floor joints so that they are flush with the top of the rim joist.

3 Use a framing square to make sure that each 2x6 joist is perfectly square to the rim joints. Once the floor decking is installed, you will depend on this standard spacing to determine your nailing schedule.

5 Once sheathing is installed, square it up flush to the outside of the rim joists and snap chalk lines to establish guiding lines to help you locate where to screw the deck in place.

6 Using chalk lines as your guide, drive 2½-in. coated screws to attach the floor to the joists. Place screws every 6 in. around the perimeter and every 8 in. in the interior of the sheet.

SMART TIP **7**

Mark joist locations on the outside of both rim joists. Use these marks to run a chalk line across the floor sheathing to aid in attaching the floor to the floor joists.

Gable Potting Shed

The Walls

Wall framing is fun and remarkably easy to master for a simple structure like this 8 × 10-foot shed. The four walls of this shed can be easily framed, sheathed, and erected in one day. It's best to do this work with two people, because lifting a 10-foot wall that's been framed and sheathed will strain even a strong back. But it can be done solo. (If you're working alone, consider erecting the framed wall and sheathing it, one sheet at a time, after you have erected and plumbed the frame.)

FRAMING OPTIONS

Because this shed will never be insulated, the walls are framed with 2×4s, spaced 16 inches on center. To maintain the spacing, see "Laying Out the Walls," on page 72. If you intend to insulate your shed or want added structural stability (especially against high wind), use 2×6 studs framed 24 inches on center because the added depth will provide more room for insulation.

Sheathing. The sheathing is ½-inch CDX plywood, which is a low-grade and inexpensive plywood that is rough on both sides. It is not a suitable finish material. CDX affords more than enough structural stability against racking (wobbly side-to-side motion) of a building, but there is no need to glue the CDX sheathing to the wall studs as we did with the floor. Just nail it every 6 inches around the perimeter and every 8 inches along the studs in the interior of each sheet. There is no need to use screws, though they offer a better wood-to-wood connection.

Windows and Doors. Do not precut rough openings before nailing the sheathing to the stud walls, whether you install sheathing with the walls lying on the floor deck or erect. It is very easy to cut out the rough openings once the walls are erected and sheathed. To create indicator points, drill through from the inside of the shed at the corners of the rough opening. You can then run chalk lines from mark to mark to frame the openings. Then plunge-cut with a circular or reciprocating saw.

FRAMING CONNECTORS

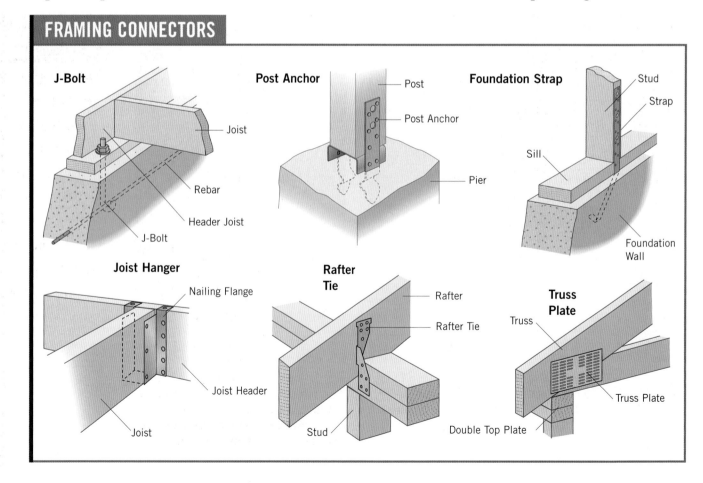

Framing the Walls

1 With a 10-ft.-long 2x4 soleplate set in place near the edge of the floor, mark off 16-in. on-center lines to guide the placement of studs.

2 Drive home two nails per stud to connect studs to the top and bottom plates. End nailing ensures a good stud to plate connection.

3 Sheathe stud walls while they sit on the floor deck by spacing nails every 6 in. around the perimeter and every 8 in. in the interior.

4 Overlap the sheathing 2 in. so that when the wall is erected, the overlap covers and protects the connection between the soleplate, the floor decking, and the rim joist.

SMART TIP 7

Nails and screws usually do an adequate job of attaching one framing member to another, but for added strength, use one of the framing connectors shown opposite

Gable Potting Shed

Framing the Walls

5 With a brace in place, you can move the wall back and forth until you achieve plumb. When erecting first walls, have temporary 2x4 braces ready to support the wall once it is plumb.

6 When laying out a wall, a rough opening is defined by a king stud and a jack stud. The king stud extends from the soleplate to the top plate, but the jack stud supports a horizontal header that defines the top of the rough opening.

8 To determine the corners of an opening, use a 1-in. spade bit to drill through from the inside at the four corners of the rough opening. With a 1-in. hole at each corner, it's easy to "connect the dots" with a reciprocating or circular saw and remove the section.

9 The corners of a rough opening can be cleaned up with a power saber saw. A ratty corner that isn't square will block the smooth installation of a window.

7 Nail king and jack studs in place, just as you would any other stud. Note that the jack stud needs to bear against the horizontal header that defines the top of the rough opening. Otherwise it will be hard to nail firmly.

Ventilation

A gable vent will help keep the shed cool and expel stale air from inside the shed. To install the vent, mark and plunge-cut a rough opening at the center of the gable-end wall. There is no need to frame a rough opening. A vent is light enough to be glued and screwed directly to the sheathing.

10 After rough openings are cut out, the sheathing can be removed and saved for other parts of the project. A good, clean rough opening is essential for proper placement of windows and doors.

11 Nail or screw through the soleplate, but don't nail the soleplate where doorways occur as you will remove this section to install the door.

SMART TIP **7**

When setting up a brace or "kicker," drive a nail almost all the way through the brace so that you can set the brace with one hammer blow once the wall is plumb.

7 Gable Potting Shed

Framing the Walls

12 Position studs 16 in. apart, even when they do not run all the way to the top plate. As you sheathe the structure, this standard spacing of 16 in. on center will allow sheathing to break directly on studs.

13 Even though studs must occur at 16 in. on center along the wall, rough openings may call for studs to occur at nonstandard intervals.

16 Once a stud wall is in place, nail the end studs into the end studs of the adjacent walls, at least every 12 in. Use a 4-ft. level to check for plumb as you work.

17 With the stud wall plumbed and nailed into adjacent walls, nail through the soleplate into the rim joist for a good connection. Do not depend on nailing through the floor decking alone to establish a sound framing connection.

14 Nail a stop board on the outside of the stud walls you have lifted into place. When adjacent walls are erected, this stop will keep the new wall from toppling over.

15 Erect walls so that they are plumb and square. One person can easily lift an 8 x 10-ft. 2x4 wall without sheathing in place.

18 On unsheathed walls, attach ½-in. plywood sheathing. Drive nails every 6 in. on the perimeter of the sheet and every 8 in. in the interior.

19 Once the four walls are erected and sheathed, tie the walls together by installing a second top plate that overlaps adjacent walls at the corners. Drive two nails for each stud bay.

SMART TIP **7**

Plywood sheathing provides stability but also adds a lot of weight to a wall. If you're working alone, consider installing the sheathing after you have lifted the framed wall into position.

Gable Potting Shed

Roof Framing

The geometry and math of roof framing can boggle the minds of mere mortals. But for a simple gable roof like the one on this shed, you can avoid all the math by setting the ridgeboard, marking and cutting a "master rafter" by holding and marking a 2×6 in place, and then using the master to cut the remaining rafters. Note that in this shed design, the ridgeboard is 12 feet long and hangs beyond both end walls to create 1-foot gable overhangs. (See "Gable Framing," page 77.)

Getting Started Though rafter framing is the most challenging aspect of this shed project, it can be managed by breaking down the steps. First, using a 2×4, place a brace board at each end of the shed. The braces run from the ground to a height 4 feet above the top plate. Position the poles so that the edge of each pole is ¾ inch to the right of the midpoint of the shed wall as you stand facing the wall. In other words, the two braces should be on opposite sides of the midpoint. (Compare photos 1 and 2.)

Attach the ridgeboard flush with the tops of the braces. Make sure the ridgeboard is set between the two poles. If the poles are plumb, the ridgeboard should be level and directly above the midpoint of the shed. Nonetheless, check the ridgeboard for level; a ridge with even a 1-inch slope across 10 feet will look out of whack to the naked eye. Mark the ridgeboard for 16-inch-on-center rafter locations.

Adding Rafters Once the ridgeboard is set, hold the master rafter in place. Make sure its butt end entirely bears on the top plate and that its end grain entirely bears on the ridgeboard. This will ensure that any loads on the roof, including snow and wind loads, are properly supported by the entire rafter at its touch points.

With the master rafter as your template, gang-cut the remaining rafters. Then install two rafters at either end of the ridgeboard. The rafters should bear directly over the studs. Apply roof sheathing. (See "Roof Sheathing," page 91.) Install roof sheathing so that you create an 18-inch overhang at the eaves.

Framing the Roof

1 With braces installed to hold the ridgeboard, temporarily nail the ridgeboard flush with the tops of the braces. Just one nail at each end is all that is required at this point.

4 Toenail the rafters to the top plate, nailing at least one nail in from each side. A band of wall sheathing will help to stabilize these rafters.

2 Check the ridgeboard for level. Because the ridge beam is attached to each brace by just one nail, you can make adjustments with ease. Also check to make sure the ridge rises 4 ft. above the top plate.

3 Before removing the braces, set the end rafters in place to stabilize the ridgeboard. The end rafters should be flush against the end of the top plates so that sheathing is flush to the stud walls and rafters.

5 Gable studs will fill in the triangle created by the gable-end rafters. These gable studs will provide a nailing surface 16 in. on center for the sheathing.

6 Check gable studs for plumb, but note that the gable-end studs are not truly a structural component of the wall; these studs serve as a nailing surface for gable sheathing.

SMART TIP 7

By placing the ridgeboard 4 feet above the top plate, you can sheathe the gable-end with a single sheet of plywood.

Gable Potting Shed

Doors and Windows

Wrapping your shed in a semipermeable house wrap, like Tyvek or Typar, is a good idea. House wrap isn't that expensive and is easy to install, and it provides a wind shield while allowing moisture that accumulates inside the shed to migrate to the outside. House wrap is especially good at sealing up rough openings before windows and doors are inserted. For best results, wrap the material around all rough openings.

Installing windows and doors in the shed provides temporary protection against the weather. But note that plywood, even with house wrap covering it, is not designed for sustained contact with the elements. So even after installing house wrap and inserting windows and doors, move directly to the installation of permanent siding and roofing to fully weatherproof the new building.

Doors. For a project like this, use prehung doors. In fact, it may be a good idea to find a door you like and use its measurements to create the rough opening size.

It takes advanced carpentry skills to build a doorjamb from stock lumber. Prehung doors are affordable, but more important, they have factory edges and quality connections. You won't regret installing a prehung door, but you may well curse the day you decided to build a doorjamb from scratch to save $100.

Windows. Though many windows come with brick molding and factory-made jambs, you do not need that style of finished window for a shed. You can save money by buying a window unit without exterior trim. Slide the window unit into the rough opening; make sure it is plumb and level, using shims if necessary; and use screws to attach it directly to the studs that form the rough opening. To finish, frame the face of the window, inside and out, with 1×4 No. 2 pine stock. The trim looks good and helps to trap the window in place.

After applying trim to the windows, it is a good idea to nail up the 1×4 trim on the gable and the eaves.

Installing Doors

1 Roll out house wrap so it is taut, and staple it in place every 12 in. or so. Overlap courses by 6 in. Once you start a course, run it as long as possible, wrapping it all the way around the shed.

4 With the rough opening crisply defined by taut house wrap stapled inside and out, install the prehung door and shim it behind each hinge. Nail through the brick molding, and nail directly through the shims to connect the doorjamb with the framing.

and Windows

2 For rough openings, use a razor knife to cut an "X" pattern in the house wrap. Don't overcut the wrap at the corners because that defeats the sealing effect of the wrap after the window is inserted.

3 Once the house wrap has been cut in an "X" pattern, fold or roll it back neatly, and staple it to the side of the studs that define the rough opening.

5 Once a window is inserted in a rough opening, shim it with cedar shingles until it is plumb and level. Drill through the shims to create a solid connection between the window, the shims, and the framing.

6 Later, you will trim windows with 1x4 No. 2 pine. Using galvanized finishing nails, fasten the trim to the shed by nailing through the sheathing into the framing.

SMART TIP 7

To get the full benefit of house wrap, run it around corners instead of stopping at the edges of a wall. Overlap the corners by at least 6 inches.

Gable Potting Shed

Siding and Trim

When it is time to trim and side your shed, you can really start to envision the finished project. Trim out the shed before you add siding because the siding will abut the trim, creating nice clean lines.

For trimming corners, around windows, and the rakes and eaves, use 1×4 No. 2 pine. Though this grade has some knots, the knots can be sealed with a sealer, and you will save the substantial cost of using clear (knot-free) pine. For a really smooth finish, sand the boards with 100-grit sandpaper before sealing the knots, and then apply two coats of exterior semigloss latex paint. (For a really smooth finish, sand between coats of paint.) It is highly advisable to paint the trim boards before you install them, even if you have to go back to touch up scuffs and hammer marks. Painting trim boards in place is time-consuming, especially around cedar siding, where you have to cut in along the edge of the shingles.

Attach the rake and eave trim by screwing down through the roof sheating. For the eave trim, rip a 45-degree bevel along the edge of the board so that it fits neatly under the roof sheathing. Be sure to level and plumb trim boards, because even a small variation from level or plumb can be picked up by the naked eye.

There is no need to glue corner-board trim, because you would be gluing the boards just to the house wrap—not the sheathing.

The Roof

Roofing is tricky when you have to contend with valleys and odd angles where roof planes meet. But with a gable roof, like the one on this shed, installing three-tab asphalt shingles is a cinch, even for beginners. First, install #10 roofing felt (very lightweight tar paper) to cover all the roof sheathing. If you are going to install shingles right away, this roofing felt can be held in place with staples or roofing nails. But if you are not installing shingles immediately, attach the roofing felt with circular nail-in-place fasteners designed just for this task (available where you

Attaching Trim

1 Prepaint all trim boards; you can touch up scuffs later. First, sand the boards, and then seal the knots. Set up trim boards on sawhorses, with 2x4 outriggers, so you can use a roller to paint lots of boards at once.

buy shingles). This gives the felt more holding power in strong winds, but it is best to apply roofing as soon as possible.

As you install roofing felt, you may want to nail in place temporary cleats as a safety measure when shingling. These can be removed as you work on the roof.

Once the roof felt is in place, install 4-inch drip edge. Drip edge really tidies up the roof edge, hiding the ratty edge where the roofing felt laps the end of the roof sheathing. Trim the drip edge to length with snips, and nail it with galvanized roofing nails. The rake and soffit trim should be in place before the drip edge.

With the drip edge in place, install a course of shingles, "upside down," with the three tabs on the uphill side of the roof. The upside-down starter course protects the underside of the first true course of shingles, where the gaps occur between tabs. It used to be recommended that this upside-down shingle course be installed just across the bottom edge of the roof, but it is a better practice to run this upside-down course all the way around the perimeter of your roof.

2 The rake board is the trim piece that is attached to the underside of the gable overhang. Use construction adhesive to glue the trim into place, and attach by screwing down through the roof sheathing.

3 Exterior trim made of 1x4 No. 2 pine is ideal for most sheds. The corner boards can be mitered at the top so that they fit snugly. A little exterior-grade caulk to seal up this joint may be required.

4 Attach corner boards by using the corner of the shed as your guide. If the walls are plumb and the foundation level, the trim boards will be plumb as well. But it's always good to double-check with a 4-ft. level.

5 Attach trim to the shed wall under the overhang, using galvanized finishing nails. You can install soffit trim or leave the soffits open.

SMART TIP **7**

To seal knots, use a primer/sealer that is formulated for that purpose. Standard drywall primer will not provide a lasting seal.

Gable Potting Shed

To apply finished shingles, start in a corner, and nail a course of shingles all the way across the full length of the roof. Once that is in place, install the second course, but start the first shingle with a "half-lap" so the gaps between the tabs don't line up with the course below. This practice will require that you run the shingles temporarily "wild" at the end of the roof. Trim shingles with a sharp razor knife by cutting the underside, using the edge of the roof sheathing as your guide.

Ridge caps are made from shingles. Simply cut a 3-tab asphalt shingle into three separate tabs. Each tab is a ridge cap. Install ridge caps by leaving exposed just the granular aspect of the shingle. For the final ridge cap, cut it in half widthwise so that you are nailing in place just the granular half of the shingle. Dab roofing adhesive on the nailheads left exposed on this last "half-tab" ridge cap. To get a good finish on ridge caps and avoid bulging, trim the part of the shingle that will be covered (the nongranular half of the tab) so that it forms an "A" shape. The A-shape allows the next shingle to fold over it without creating a bulge.

Roofing the Shed

1 Apply roofing felt across the entire roof before shingling. Overlap any seams by 6 in., and trim the edges with a sharp razor knife. Stapling will hold the roofing felt in place if you are installing shingles right away.

4 Before installing finished shingles, install an upside-down "under course" of shingles—with the tabs facing in—all the way around the perimeter of the roof. This protects the gap beneath the tabs of the first course.

5 As you work up from the bottom of the roof, each successive course of shingles must have the tabs staggered by half a tab. This ensures that the gaps between tabs in a shingle course do not line up with the gaps between tabs of the shingle course below.

2 Along the gable end and along the soffit, a 4-in. drip edge really adds a nice neat look to the edge of the roof. Note that the rake and soffit trim boards must be in place for the drip edge to be installed properly.

3 Trim drip edge with sharp snips. There is no need to miter the corners of the drip edge. The drip-edge pieces simply overlap one another. Nail them in place with standard galvanized roofing nails.

6 Allow shingles to hang temporarily "wild" over the edge of the roof, and then trim them by cutting with a sharp razor knife across the underside of the shingle. Do not cut the shingles from the top, granular side. It will dull the razor very quickly.

7 Ridge caps are made by cutting up the three-tab shingles into three individual tabs. Overlap ridge caps so that just the granular half of the tab is exposed. Dab nailheads with roofing cement.

SMART TIP 7

When roofing, especially in the heat, avoid walking on the shingles. They are remarkably fragile. Use soft shoes, like sneakers. Better yet, don't walk on them and work off a ladder positioned so it lays flush against the roof.

Gable Potting Shed

Building Steps

The shed's entryway can be as elaborate as a stairway with handrails or as simple as a platform made of pressure-treated wood. In all cases, level the rim joists, just as you did with the rim joists for the shed's foundation. Build a box to size; then attach 2x6 pressure-treated planks to the joists.

When positioning 2x6 pressure-treated decking planks, leave enough room between them—about ½ in.—to allow standing water to drain.

Finishing the Shed

1 Siding with cedar shingles is fun, though time-consuming, because as each course ends, you may have to custom-cut shingles with a razor knife to bring the course flush up against the corner boards.

4 Some shingle courses may have shingles that are just 4 in. tall. These must be nailed in place with galvanized finishing nails because there will be no course laid on top to cover the exposed nailheads.

2 Getting the first course level is crucial. After the first course is in place, measure up to the bottom of the next course, and this course-to-course distance must be maintained for the entire structure.

3 Shingling under windows may require that you cut off the tops of some shingles to make them fit. Trim as needed to maintain the exposure established below.

5 Seal knots on all pine trim because the sap from knots will invariably bleed through most finish paints, leaving unsightly brown circles. You will have to discard the brush you use for sealant, so pick an old one you don't mind throwing away.

SMART TIP **7**

Never trim cedar shingles from the bottom because the thickness at the bottom of the shingles must match across the entire course of shingles.

Gable Potting Shed

8

Attached Tool Shed

Building an Attached Shed

One person can easily build the attached shed shown in this chapter over a weekend for around $300 in material costs. If you have all the materials on hand and precut the lumber and sheathing, you can easily build this shed from scratch in one long day, even working alone.

Though only 2 feet deep, this structure is 6 feet wide, which produces 12 square feet of floor space. That may not seem like much, but the shed rises 8 feet in the back, providing ample room for 6-foot-long shelves that span the shed from side to side. Or you can install shorter shelves and provide an area to hang or stand tools upright.

Firm Foundation. Constructing the floor and foundation for this shed is simplified by the fact that the

structure is attached at the back to an existing structure. In this case, the existing structure is a horse barn, but you can build your shed on the back or side of your house or on a garage wall. The back corners of the shed do not need support blocks of any kind. You could, of course, support the back corners with concrete blocks as shown in the illustration opposite.

For the front of the shed, 4-inch solid blocks serve to support the frame. Since the shed shown here was built under a sheltered area, there was no risk of frost heaving, so there is no gravel beneath the cap blocks. In most other situations, gravel is required beneath the foundation blocks to provide drainage.

Framing. Framing this attached structure is a cinch. But to make it even easier, we prefabricated two standing frame trusses in a workshop to serve as the end walls. Made of 2×4s lying flat, this wall frame was created with galvanized corner braces to add stability. The two identical frames are screwed to perimeter ledger boards (2×4s) attached to the plywood back. This approach to framing the sidewalls saved a great deal of site cutting. Of course, you have the option of building the frames on site. Siding consists of T1-11 siding. The same material is used on the doors as well. The size of the sidewalls allows you to cut the sheathing for each wall from a single sheet of siding.

Roofing. The roof angle is easy to determine because the frames for the walls consist of an 8-foot stud for the back wall and a 6-foot stud in the front, creating a 45-degree angle. You can hold the rafters in place to judge their length.

The roof sheathing of ½–inch CDX plywood that is topped with standard three-tab asphalt shingles. To help keep the inside of your shed dry, install a section of aluminum flashing under the last course of shingles or siding on the existing structure and over the juncture of the shed roof and the existing building.

An attached shed like this is a great project to build your confidence, as it is easy to undo mistakes and there is no heavy lifting, making it an ideal project to tackle on your own.

MATERIALS LIST

FRAMING

4	4" solid concrete blocks	
15 pcs.	2x4 8'	SPF
14 pcs.	1x4 8'	No. 2 pine
3 sheets	½" CDX plywood	
3 sheets	4x8 T1-11 siding	
8	galvanized corner braces (for the frame trusses)	
10d nails		
2½" coated or galvanized wood screws		
2½" finishing nails		
screws		

ROOFING

1 bundle	3-tab roof shingles	
2 pcs.	8' x 4" drip edge	
⅞" roofing nails		

FINISHING

1 gal.	white exterior semigloss paint	
1 qt.	knot sealer	
1	galvanized handle	
2	slide bolts	
4	heavy duty galvanized hinges	

Attached Tool Shed

Cover the back wall with perforated hardboard to serve as a base for hanging small hand and garden tools.

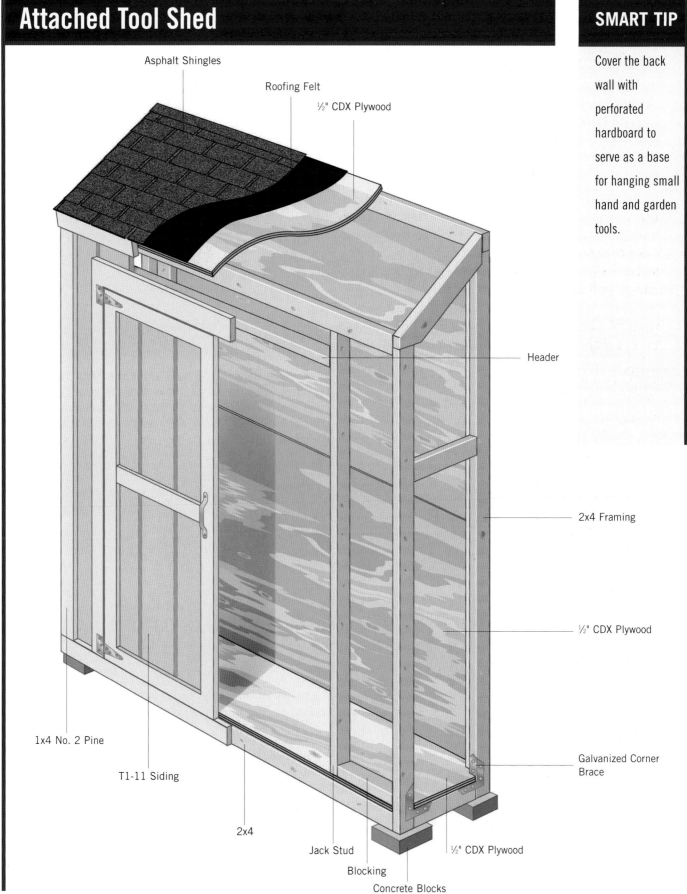

Asphalt Shingles

Roofing Felt

½" CDX Plywood

Header

2x4 Framing

½" CDX Plywood

Galvanized Corner Brace

1x4 No. 2 Pine

T1-11 Siding

2x4

Jack Stud

Blocking

Concrete Blocks

½" CDX Plywood

Framing

This attached shed is framed entirely with 2×4s. Because there is so little distance to span, even the rafters are 2×4s.

As a first step in framing the attached shed, cover a 6-foot-wide by 8-foot-high section of the adjoining structure with ½-inch CDX plywood, which will become the back wall of the shed. The plywood back of the attached shed is made up of two sheets of plywood, each trimmed to 6 feet and stacked one on top of the other. You can have these precut at a home center to make sure your cuts are true.

Once the plywood back is level and plumb, attach a 2×4 border around its perimeter, but on the sides, back off the edge of the plywood by the thickness of a 2×4—or 1½ inches. This will allow you to attach the framed walls to the perimeter 2×4s securely. Install the 2×4s on the top and bottom flush with the edge of the plywood.

Support the front of the shed with concrete blocks. Make sure they are level before adding the sidewalls.

Framing

1 After defining the back of the shed with ½-in. CDX plywood, install perimeter 2x4s, but back off from the edge of the plywood by 1½ in. This will provide a good attachment area for the wall frames when it is time to install them.

4 After the foundation blocks are set, place the side-wall frames in position. It is crucial to get these frames plumb and level. Use screws to attach the frame trusses to the perimeter 2x4s that are mounted on the plywood base.

5 With the sidewalls in place and attached to the 2x4s on the plywood base, connect the two walls using a 93-in.-long 2x4. This will form part of the shed's floor framing. Install another 2x4 between the two walls flush with the top of the 6-ft. front stud.

Sheds attached to the house or garage should be sided with the same material used on the existing structure.

2 The 2x4 at the base of the plywood that forms the back of the shed can be installed flush to the bottom of the plywood base. Use 2½-in. coated or galvanized wood screws.

3 Set the blocks to support the front wall of the attached shed. The base of the back wall does not require blocks because you will attach the shed to the existing structure.

6 Attach T1-11 siding to the sidewalls. Because these walls are just 2 ft. wide, you will only need to fasten the siding at the perimeter. The 1x4 trim that will cover all edges of the shed will hide the screw heads.

7 T1-11 siding is as easy to install as plywood, yet it comes prepainted and it doesn't need to be covered with another form of siding, such as clapboard or cedar shingles. For sheds that will be finished with clapboard or cedar shingles, use ½-in. plywood as a sheathing.

Installing Flooring and Roofing

1 Given that the floor of this attached shed will probably hold tools and other heavy items, such as large bags of potting soil, it's a good idea to reinforce the floor with 2x4 joists. Divide the floor space into thirds.

2 Cut a 69 x 24-in. section of ½-in. CDX plywood for the floor of the shed. Attach it to the frame using galvanized screws spaced every 6 in. along the front and back of the shed. Drive at least two screws into each of the joists.

5 Using a table saw, rip a piece of 1x4 No. 2 pine with a 45-deg. bevel, and place it under the plywood roof deck. As with all trim, it is best to prime and paint the trim before installation because it is hard to maintain clean lines when painting trim boards in place.

6 Because the roof deck has some spring in it and the fasteners will be hidden by the roof shingles, drive screws, rather than nails, through the plywood roof deck to attach the trim.

Use ¾-in. plywood for the shed floor if you plan to store extremely heavy items.

3 Rafters this short are easy to cut, with little math required. The angles are simple 45-deg. cuts. Start with an over-long rafter, and experiment with lengths until you get a rafter that fits. Then use that as a model rafter to cut two more—for a total of three.

4 Install ½-in. CDX plywood as the roof sheathing. The roof is 104 in. wide, so you will need two sheets of plywood. Attach them using 2-in. galvanized screws.

7 With the trim boards installed around the entire roof, install drip edge. The best way to install drip edge is to hold a long section in place, and nip it with snips to indicate the cut lines. Remove and cut the section to length, and then nail the cut section in place.

8 Roof the shed using three-tab asphalt shingles. Just as with a typical house roof, run an underlying course of shingles upside-down around the roof perimeter. This protects the roof deck at the edges of the roof.

The Front Wall

Build the doors by constructing two 26 × 54-in 2×4 frames with center blocking, and then adding T1-11 sheathing. Attach the sheathing to the frames by driving screws every 6 inches around the perimeter and every 8 inches or so through the blocking. It is important to properly fasten the T1-11 to the door frame and blocking because the door covering will sag if not properly attached and supported. Trim out the doors before they are installed, as the door hardware will be attached directly to the trim.

To frame the door opening, install a 6-inch-long 2×4 laid flat against each end stud on the front of the shed. Nail a stud on each side of the opening, fastening them to the floor plates and screwing them to the upper horizontal cross member. Once studs are in place, install a 2×4 header. The height of the header is crucial because it will establish the top of the rough opening for the front doors. Install the header at a height that equals the height of the door plus ½-inch clearance at the bottom and top of the doors.

The Front Wall

1 Create frames for the doors using 2x4s. Install blocking at the midpoint because the T1-11 siding that forms the door sheathing would otherwise sag without this support. Test fit the doors before they are sheathed.

4 The header at the top of the rough opening should be 55 in. from the floor of the shed. Check for level. If it isn't level, it will pinch the shed doors when they open and close.

5 T1-11 siding can be attached to the face of the shed with screws driven around the perimeter. Because the shed will be trimmed with 1x4 pine, the screw heads will be hidden.

Even on a small structure, it is sometimes necessary to add blocking to provide needed nailing surfaces.

2 With the 2x4 frame completed, lay in place a section of T1-11 siding, cut exactly to the dimensions of the door's 2x4 frame. Nail or screw it around the perimeter of the 2x4 frame every 6 inches. This helps protect the door against racking.

3 Frame the rough opening. Use short 2x4 plates (blocks) as spacers at the base of the jack stud. These plates provide a good place to drive screws or nails.

6 Attach an 18-in.-wide strip of T1-11 siding across the top of the shed's front. Note that trim will cover any rough edges or screw heads.

7 Nail up primed and painted 1x4 No. 2 pine trim, and touch up the nailheads with paint. Use galvanized finishing nails or finishing screws.

Add the Doors

With the rough opening of the door established, finish sheathing and adding trim to the face of the shed. Begin installing the doors by holding them in place and marking the locations for the strap hinges. These are surface-mounted hinges that do not require any cutting or mortising for installation.

The best way to approach this is to place a piece of ½-inch plywood on the floor of the shed as a temporary spacer to help you establish bottom clearance for the door. This is a necessary step to ensure that the doors will swing open freely. Mark the locations for the strap hinges. Plan on a hinge at each corner. If the shed you build is taller, you may want to plan on an additional hinge in the middle of the door. To install them, drive screws into the shed's framing.

To give your shed a finished look, pick door handles and latches that have the same finish as the one on the hinges. The handles and latches are easier to install with the doors held in a closed position.

Attach the Doors

1 There should be a ½-in. clearance at the top and bottom of the doors. At the bottom of the door, establish the clearance by setting the door on a ½-in. plywood spacer.

4 A slide bolt at the top and bottom of the doors will help secure the door. Note that there is a trim board attached to the door on the left that overlaps the door on the right, covering any gap between the doors. The slide bolt that holds the door closed is attached to the center trim board.

5 Rather than using nails, use finishing screws that have very small heads. The screw heads can be easily countersunk in the soft pine trim, covered with caulk, and touched up with white paint.

Create a clean look by installing a piece of trim on one of the doors so that it overlaps the seam between doors.

2 With the doors temporarily shimmed and held in place with spacers, check that the doors are level. Set the hinges by drilling through the trim. Use 2-in. screws, long enough to penetrate the trim and the framing beneath. This will help stabilize the door.

3 Attaching the handle is a simple matter of centering it on the trim that is attached to the face of the door. Use a torpedo level to make sure the handle is plumb.

6 Even though it is easy to skip ahead without using a level, be sure each piece of trim is level and plumb before fastening it to the shed.

Building a Small Locker-Type Shed

1 To create a small shed that will not have any ground contact, define the outline of the shed with 2x4s. You can make the shed any size you wish. This one measures 3 x 5 feet.

2 Use galvanized corner braces to frame the sidewalls. Attach them using galvanized screws to the frame you attached in the previous step.

5 Attach short ledgers to all four sides of the inside of the shed frame. These will provide an attachment surface for the shed floor. Install them flush with the top of the floor frame.

6 Install ½-in. plywood cut to size to form the floor of the shed. The floor is simply screwed directly to the ledger boards.

To be safe, install a lock on your shed, especially if you are storing pool or lawn chemicals, or sharp tools.

3 Attach a ledger to the main structure. The ledger should be the width of the attached shed. Again, use galvanized screws.

4 Install diagonal braces, or struts, to support the shed. Hold a 2x4 in place to determine the length and angle for cutting.

7 Sheathe the attached shed with T1-11 siding (or plywood as a substrate for clapboard or cedar siding). Because the attached shed will be trimmed out on its edges, use screws because the trim boards will cover the heads.

8 Hang a 2x4 framed door similar to the one shown on page 174 but sized to fit the smaller shed. (See page 173 for instructions on how to finish the roof.)

Building a
Shed Kit

Shed Kit Components

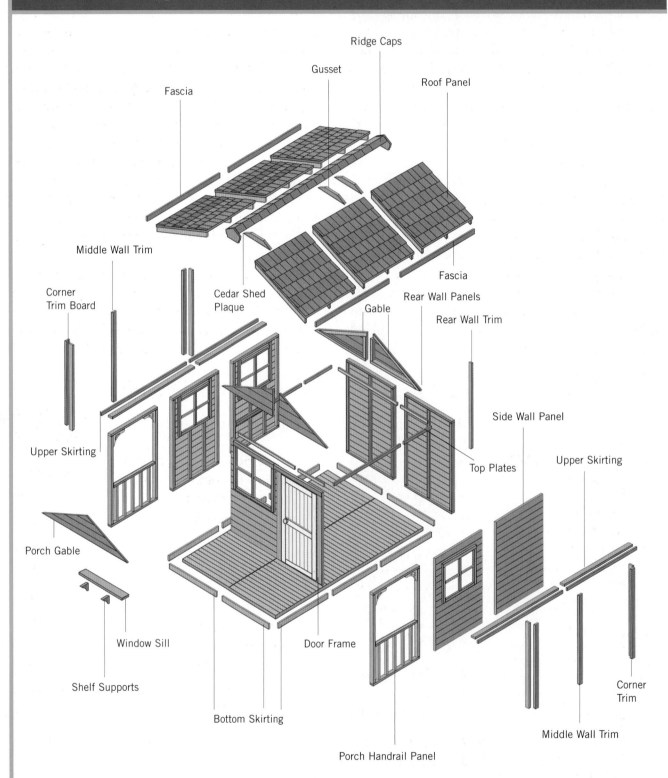

Ridge Caps

Gusset

Roof Panel

Fascia

Middle Wall Trim

Corner Trim Board

Cedar Shed Plaque

Fascia

Rear Wall Panels

Gable

Rear Wall Trim

Upper Skirting

Side Wall Panel

Upper Skirting

Top Plates

Porch Gable

Window Sill

Door Frame

Corner Trim

Shelf Supports

Middle Wall Trim

Bottom Skirting

Porch Handrail Panel

Assembling a Shed Kit

Shed kits, like the one shown in this chapter, are made up of prefabricated components that you assemble on site. Our shed is one of the products offered by Spirit Elements of Boulder, Colorado. It was shipped to our site in 4 × 4-foot sections. The kit included the wall and ceiling panels, a complete trim package with all the boards labeled for identification, and all the screws and nails needed for assembly.

If you have ever stick-built a shed or other outbuilding, you will find assembling a shed kit remarkably easy. The roofs on most kits do not even need to be shingled. Roof panels are preshingled. You simply join the panels using metal strips supplied by the manufacturer. The strips are covered with extra shingles. You can take delivery of your kit in the morning and—with a little luck—be sipping a cool drink on the porch at sunset the same day.

Working Arrangement. Two people, or even one strong person, can easily manage most of the kit components. If you can lift and manage a single sheet of ½-inch plywood, you can easily handle the pieces from a typical kit. The only time you may need a helper is when you install the roof panels. Positioning them properly, holding them in place, and fastening them all at the same time can be a real challenge for just one person.

Kits do not come with foundation systems. That part of the project is usually your responsibility, and you have a choice among all the types discussed in Chapter 3 "Foundation Types," pages 52 to 65. The shed shown here has a foundation system of 4-inch concrete blocks set on crushed stone.

Prepare for the assembly of your kit by arranging for access to electric power or having your cordless drill batteries all charged up—most kits are assembled with screws. Though it goes without saying, read the instructions carefully.

MATERIALS LIST

FLOOR AND WALLS

- 4 floor panels 46½" x 72⁵⁄₁₆"
- 2 window wall 46½" x 74⅞"
- 4 rear and side wall (a) 46" x 73¼"
- 1 front wall 46½" x 74⅞"
- 1 door frame and door
- 2 porch rail section 73⁵⁄₁₆" x 45"
- 2 front and rear wall top side plate (c)1" x 3" x 87⅞"
- 2 top side plate (a) 1" x 3" x 72⁵⁄₁₆"
- 2 top side plate (b) 1" x 3" x 25⅞"
- 4 rim joists 2" x 3" x 46½"

ROOFING

- 4 gable 55⅜" x 20"
- 1 porch gable 76" x 16"
- 2 center roof 48¾" x 60"
- 2 back roof 49½" x 60"
- 2 porch roof 49½" x 60"
- 4 gusset (a) 2" x 3" x 42"
- 1 gusset (b) 2" x 3" x 22"
- 18 (bundle) ridge caps
- 1 roofing felt
- 20 metal flashing

TRIM ELEMENTS

- 4 shutter 6" x 27"
- 2 flower box 8½" x 22"
- 4 top skirting ½" x 3" x 45"
- 2 back top skirting ½" x 4½" x 45"
- 2 bottom skirting ½" x 3" x 45"
- 2 bottom/side porch skirting 1" x 4" x 45¾"
- 2 bottom/front porch skirting 1" x 4" x 47¼"
- 4 soffit ½" x 4" x 50"
- 4 corner board 1" x 4" x 77½"
- 1 left side corner bead 1" x 2" x 73 ⁵⁄₁₆"
- 2 corner trim 1" x 2" x 77½"
- 3 side middle trim 1" x 2" x 77½"
- 1 front gable trim 1" x 2" x 17¼"
- 1 back gable trim 1" x 2" x 22"
- 4 fascia 1" x 4" x 73⅛"

WINDOWS

- 4 header 2" x 3" x 46½"
- 2 track for window 2" x 2" x 75¼"
- 1 sliding window
- 1 window sill plate
- 2 shelf support 2" x 6"
- 2 plaques

HARDWARE

- screws 3"
- screws 2"
- finishing nails 1¾"
- ridge cap nails 2"
- roofing felt nails 1"
- 1 door lock
- 2 sliding window barrel bolts

SMART TIP

Read the instructions. Some kit components look identical to others, but they are not interchangeable. Small differences mean they can be used in only one place.

Starting the Project

Shed kits are no different from any other building in at least one respect: problems with the foundation, such as out-of-square or sloped blocks or unsteady footings, will plague the entire project. Foundation problems will express themselves in the finished structure with windows that don't close squarely or doors that need to be trimmed to coax them into position. Although it is tempting to just jump in and start screwing together kit components, level your foundation precisely before starting in on the kit.

Building Details. Although most kit designs do not strictly follow period architectural styles, some kits include components, such as window trim and other accessories, that adhere to a specific architectural detail. In addition, many kits are not made using full-dimension 2×4 lumber. Instead, manufacturers use 2×3 framing or even smaller structural elements. The components may seem flimsy at first, but once they are all in place and bracing one another, you'll find that most kits are fairly well engineered. They may not have the stability that a 2×4 or 2×6 structure has when sheathed with ½-inch plywood, but they will do the job of keeping the rain and snow off your stored items.

Kit Delivery and Storage

Kits are usually packed on pallets and dropped off by a large truck. Arrange to be on location when the delivery truck arrives. If the truck doesn't have a forklift, you may have to cut the packing straps and take the pieces of the kit off the truck one at a time. In any event, establish a holding area near your worksite where you can place the kit pieces. Arrange beforehand to place the sections on scrap lumber to keep them off of the ground.

If you can convince the truck driver to wait a few minutes before unloading, dig into the pallet to find the kit assembly guide. Determine the order of assembly for each kit section, and place them near your worksite in that order. This will save you from having to double-handle the pieces or restack them later.

Floor Systems

1 Four-in. concrete blocks placed 6 ft. apart provide the foundation for this shed kit. We built on a slight rise, so the high point of the foundation required just one block. Stacked blocks receive a bead of construction adhesive.

4 One person can easily manage the floor sections. By using the level foundation blocks as your guide, you can align the sections without any trouble.

2 Use a straight 2x4 and a 4-ft. level to make sure the foundation is level. A foundation that is not true will cause you headaches throughout the entire assembly process.

3 The floor consists of four separate panels. Screw a ledger into each section. This ledger is used to join the panels together by screwing down through the floor into it.

5 To hold the floor panels together, screw down through the floor section you want to connect into the ledger that is attached to the adjoining section.

SMART TIP   **9**

Many manufacturers provide for Internet tracking of your kit while it is in transit to you. Ask for a tracking number when ordering.

Building a Shed Kit

Walls

1 Screw the bottom plate of the wall sections into the floor framing, just as you would screw a 2x4 wall soleplate to a floor deck. You can plumb the walls once adjacent walls are in place.

2 Erect and fasten wall sections the same way you would traditional stud walls. The fact that the wall sections are preassembled doesn't change the traditional fastening techniques used.

5 Even the door in a kit is prefabricated and needs merely to be hung by its hinges. This door was predrilled for the appropriate latch-set hardware.

6 After you have assembled all four walls, screw in place the top plates, which run the full length of the wall sections to provide even more structural support for the wall assembly.

3 When you erect and fasten adjacent walls, you can plumb all the walls using the sections you installed previously as bracing.

4 The front wall of this kit has an opening for a window and a door. As you progress to this point, be sure all the walls are plumb and the corners are square.

7 With the walls plumb and square and the top plate screwed in place to add extra bracing, place the gable-end sections to support the roof panels.

8 Trim pieces in this shed kit are used as much to give a neat over-all appearance as they are to add some degree of weatherproofing. The trim pieces cover exposed seams between shed components.

SMART TIP **9**

Many kit manufacturers offer a choice of lumber species for their products. The type of lumber you select could increase the cost of the kit.

Building a Shed Kit

The Roof

For those of you who have puzzled over shingle patterns or whacked your thumb a few too many times nailing shingles or shakes, a kit offers a unique alternative to the meticulous, tricky work of roofing. With many kits, the roof comes as preshingled modular sections, and all you do is install the sections, connecting them with supplied metal strips to keep the water from penetrating the seams. Just as with any roof you shingle, the kit will require that you put up ridge caps and some eave trim, but the process will go remarkably faster than covering a roof with individual shingles.

After the roof for this kit was installed, we placed a triangular gable section under the roof in the very front of the shed. This not only added a nice architectural element to the shed, but the gable insert served a structural function as well because it stabilized the roof sections and helped to keep them from spreading apart. Many decorative elements have a functional use as well.

Adding the Roof

1 Once you have installed the walls and screwed the triangular spacers in place on top of the end walls, you can put the roof sections in place. These are best installed by two people.

4 Forget all the hard work of cutting and nailing rail spindles. That is all done at the factory, so you can simply lift the porch framing into place and screw it securely to the shed walls and to the floor joists below.

5 With the porch framing in place, install the roof sections that form the covering for the porch. Again, this portion of the job would be much easier with a helper.

2 Bridge the seam between two sections by inserting the metal strips that came with the package. There is no need to use adhesive or caulk here because the metal strips are held in place by friction.

3 Install the ridge caps by maintaining the traditional 6-in. overlap. These cedar ridge caps had a tendency to split when nailed too aggressively, but there were plenty of extra caps in the kit.

6 Triangular sections at the gable end of the porch add a nice architectural element while serving the extra purpose of tying the end rafters together securely—like an oversized gusset.

7 Inside the shed, tie the rafters together by screwing a sturdy gusset in place. This helped to keep the rafters from spreading under their own weight or from the added weight of a wind or snow load.

SMART TIP | **9**

To aid in installing roof panels, set up scaffolding inside the shed. This will keep you from having to climb up and down a ladder.

Building a Shed Kit

Adding Trim

Though it is prudent to have a chop saw on site when assembling your shed, you probably won't end up using it on the trim package. On this kit, all the trim was precut to the proper length and clearly marked with labels as to where it should go. An ample number of appropriately sized nails were also supplied. The trim was used not only in the traditional locations—like the rake, skirt, and eaves—but also to cover seams where kit components joined together, such as where wall sections met or around the windows.

Trimming out this shed will probably be the most fun part of assembling the kit. That's because you save a remarkable amount of time by not having to measure, cut, and install each piece of trim, as one does with a stick-built structure. You can simply go to the trim package, check the label, and nail the trim piece in place. The lengths of the trim pieces are remarkably accurate. Be sure to organize the trim pieces before beginning assembly.

Adding Accessories

After you have assembled the shed, you can dress it up with accessories. Many kits come with window boxes and shelving, and you can either follow the shed designer's suggestions when locating and installing these or simply screw them into place wherever you want them to be. Don't hesitate to add your own touches as well. There is nothing to say that a shed kit has to be left as is, and you can modify it with storage features, ramps for easy entry of rolling yard equipment, stairways, additional doorways, windows, extended porches, weather vanes, or even salvaged architectural items that would really add some character to your structure. As with any building, try to match the finish material of the shed kit with whatever else you add to it. For example, if the shed is clear western red cedar, make additional window boxes and shelves out of the same species of wood, not knotty white pine. Also, tie the window boxes and shelving into the existing structural elements of the shed frame, but don't be shy about supplementing that frame with additional studs or rafter gussets if you feel you need to beef up the structure to accommodate the additions you are bringing to it.

Trim Elements

1 This shed kit contains corner boards, which you install after the wall panels are in place.

4 Trim pieces for this shed kit are clearly marked, as are the finishing nails used to install the trim. You can install the entire trim package in less than an hour.

2 Skirt boards in this kit are nicely tied into the corner boards. The trim produces a neat frame along all of the edges of the kit.

3 Trim on the eaves did not add to tightening up the building envelope, as it would have in a boxed eave on a traditional rafter roof, but it did a nice job of making the ends of the rafters appear neat.

SMART TIP | **9**

Building a Shed Kit

Before adding trim pieces, lay out the components near their locations. That way you will know whether you have everything you need before you begin installation.

5 Trimming out the windows with precut trim pieces is a cinch because the pieces simply abut at the corners, so there is no need to miter them. Not having to cut each piece of trim to exact lengths saves a great deal of measuring and cutting time.

Best-Selling Shed Plans

How Many Plans Should You Order?

Standard 8-Set Package. We've found that our 8-set package is the best value for someone who is ready to start building. Once the process begins, a number of people will require their own set of blueprints. The 8-set package provides plans for you, your builder, the subcontractors, mortgage lender, and the building department.

Minimum 5-Set Package. If you are in the bidding process, you may want to order only five sets for the bidding round and reorder additional sets as needed.

1-Set Study Package. The 1-set package allows you to review your shed plan in detail. The plan will be marked as a study print, and it is illegal to build a house from a study print alone. It is a violation of copyright law to reproduce a blueprint without permission.

Buying Additional Sets

If you require additional copies of blueprints for your shed, you can order additional sets within 60 days of the original order date at a reduced price. The cost is $45.00 for each additional set. Contact customer service for details.

Reproducible Masters

If you plan to make minor changes to one of our shed plans, you can purchase reproducible masters. Printed on vellum paper, an erasable paper that you can reproduce in a copying machine, reproducible masters allow an architect, designer, or builder to alter our plans to give you a customized shed design. This package also allows you to print as many copies of the modified plans as you need for construction.

CAD Files

CAD files are the complete set of shed plans in an electronic file format. Choose this option if there are multiple changes you wish made to the shed plans and you have a local design professional able to make the changes. Not available for all plans. Please contact our order department or visit our Web site to check the availability of CAD files for your plan.

Mirror-Reverse Sets/Right-Reading Reverse

Plans can be printed in mirror-reverse—we can "flip" plans to create a mirror image of the design. This is useful when the shed would fit your site or personal preferences if all the features were on the opposite side than shown. As the image is reversed, the lettering and dimensions will also be reversed, meaning they will read backwards. Therefore, when ordering mirror-reverse drawings, you must order at least one set of right-reading plans. A $50.00 fee per plan order will be charged for mirror-reverse (regardless of the number of mirror-reverse sets ordered). Some plans are available in right-reading reverse, this feature will show the plan in reverse, but the writing on the plan will be readable. A $150.00 fee per plan order will be charged for right-reading reverse (regardless of the number of right-reading reverse sets ordered). Please contact our order department or visit our website to check the availibility of this feature for your chosen plan.

CompleteCost Estimator

CompleteCost Estimator is a valuable tool for use in planning and constructing your new shed. It combines the detail of a materials list with line-by-line cost estimating. The result is a complete, detailed estimate—similar to a bid—that will act as a checklist for all the items you will need to select or coordinate during our building process. CompleteCost Estimator is only available for certain plans and may only be ordered with the purchase of at least five sets of shed plans. The cost is $125.00 for CompleteCost Estimator.

Materials List

Available for most of our plans, the Materials List provides you an invaluable resource in planning and estimating the cost of your shed. Each Materials List outlines the quantity, dimensions, and type of materials needed to build your shed. You will get faster, more-accurate bids from your contractors and building suppliers—and avoid paying for unused materials. A Materials List is included with each plan order.

Order Toll Free by Phone
1-800-523-6789
By Fax: 201-760-2431

Regular office hours are
8:30AM–7:30PM ET, Mon–Fri

Orders received 3PM ET, will be processed
and shipped within two business days.

Order Online
www.ultimateplans.com

Mail Your Order
Creative Homeowner
Attn: Home Plans
24 Park Way
Upper Saddle River, NJ 07458

Canadian Customers
Order Toll Free 1-800-393-1883

Mail Your Order (Canada)
Creative Homeowner Canada
Attn: Home Plans
113-437 Martin St., Ste. 215
Penticton, BC V2A 5L1

Before You Order

Our Exchange Policy

Blueprints are nonrefundable. However, should you find that the plan you have purchased does not fit your needs, you may exchange that plan for another plan in our collection within 60 days from the date of your original order. The entire content of your original order must be returned before an exchange will be processed. You will be charged a processing fee of 20% of the amount of the original order, the cost difference between the new plan set and the original plan set (if applicable), and all related shipping costs for the new plans. Contact our order department for more information. Please note: reproducible masters may only be exchanged if the package is unopened, and CAD files are nonrefundable and cannot be exchanged.

Building Codes and Requirements

At the time of creation, our plans meet the bulding code requirements published by the Building Officials and Code Administrators International, the Southern Building Code Congress International, the International Conference of Building Officials, or the Council of American Building Officials. Because building codes vary from area to area, some drawing modifications and/or the assistance of a professional designer or architect may be necessary to comply with your local codes or to accommodate specific building site conditions. We strongly advise you to consult with your local building official for information regarding codes governing your area.

Blueprint Price Schedule

Price Code	1 Set	5 Sets	Reproducible Masters	CAD	Materials List
AA	$60	$85	$125	$425	Included
BB	$85	$105	$150	$450	Included
CC	$110	$135	$175	$475	Included
DD	$135	$155	$200	$500	Included
EE	$150	$180	$230	$530	Included
FF	$190	$220	$270	$570	Included

Note: all prices subject to change

Shipping & Handling

	1-4 Sets	5-7 Sets	8+ Sets or Reproducibles	CAD
US Regular (7–10 business days)	$18	$20	$25	$25
US Priority (3–5 business days)	$25	$30	$35	$35
US Express (1–2 business days)	$40	$45	$50	$50
Canada Express (1–2 business days)	$60	$70	$80	$80
Worldwide Express (3–5 business days)	$80	$80	$80	$80

Note: all delivery times are from date the blueprint package is shipped (typically within 1-2 days of placing order).

Order Form — Please send me the following:

Plan Number: _____ **Price Code:** _____

Basic Blueprint Package

	Cost
❏ CAD File	
❏ Reproducible Masters	$_____
❏ 8-Set Plan Package	$_____
❏ 5-Set Plan Package	$_____
❏ 1-Set Study Package	$_____
❏ Additional plan sets: __ sets at $45.00 per set	$_____
❏ Print in mirror-reverse: $50.00 per order *Please call all our order department or visit our website for availibility*	$_____
❏ Print in right-reading reverse: $150.00 per order *Please call all our order department or visit our website for availibility*	$_____
Shipping (see chart above)	$_____
SUBTOTAL	$_____
Sales Tax (NJ residents only, add 6%)	$_____
TOTAL	$_____

Order Toll Free: 1-800-523-6789 By Fax: 201-760-2431
Creative Homeowner
24 Park Way
Upper Saddle River, NJ 07458

Name _____
(Please print or type)

Street _____
(Please do not use a P.O. Box)

City _____ State _____

Country _____ Zip _____

Daytime telephone (   ) _____

Fax (   ) _____
(Required for reproducible orders)

E-Mail _____

Payment ❏ Check/money order *Make checks payable to Creative Homeowner*

❏ VISA   ❏ MasterCard   ❏ American Express Cards   ❏ Discover

Credit card number _____

Expiration date (mm/yy) _____

Signature _____

Please check the appropriate box:
❏ Licensed builder/contractor   ❏ Homeowner   ❏ Renter

SOURCE CODE CA603

Garden Shed

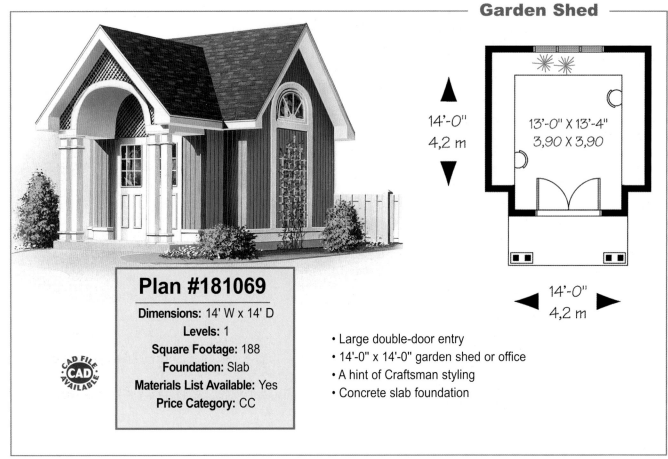

14'-0"
4,2 m

13'-0" X 13'-4"
3,90 X 3,90

14'-0"
4,2 m

Plan #181069

Dimensions: 14' W x 14' D

Levels: 1

Square Footage: 188

Foundation: Slab

Materials List Available: Yes

Price Category: CC

CAD FILE AVAILABLE

- Large double-door entry
- 14'-0" x 14'-0" garden shed or office
- A hint of Craftsman styling
- Concrete slab foundation

Dual Garden Sheds

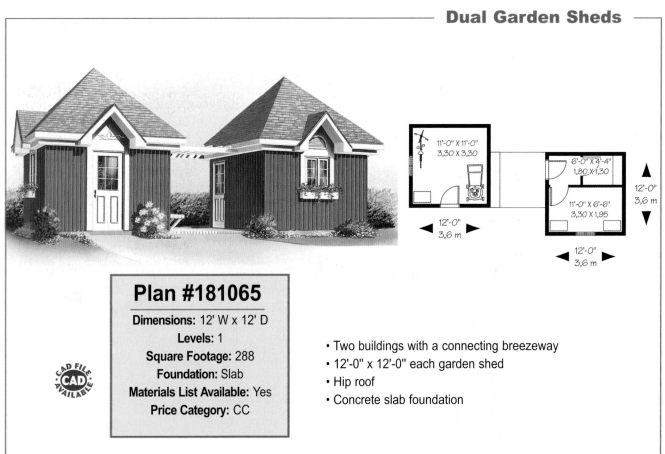

11'-0" X 11'-0"
3,30 X 3,30

6'-0" X 4'-4"
1,80 X 1,30

11'-0" X 6'-6"
3,30 X 1,95

12'-0"
3,6 m

12'-0"
3,6 m

12'-0"
3,6 m

Plan #181065

Dimensions: 12' W x 12' D

Levels: 1

Square Footage: 288

Foundation: Slab

Materials List Available: Yes

Price Category: CC

CAD FILE AVAILABLE

- Two buildings with a connecting breezeway
- 12'-0" x 12'-0" each garden shed
- Hip roof
- Concrete slab foundation

Attached Shed

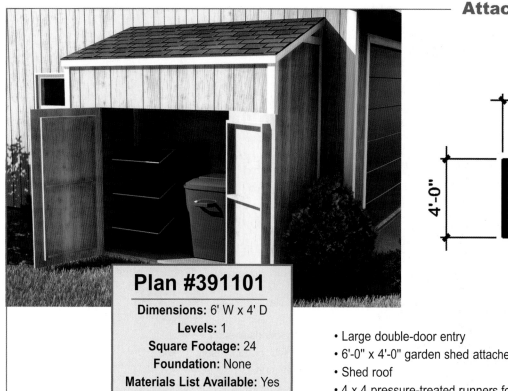

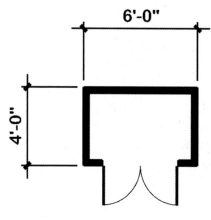

6'-0"

4'-0"

Plan #391101

Dimensions: 6' W x 4' D
Levels: 1
Square Footage: 24
Foundation: None
Materials List Available: Yes
Price Category: AA

- Large double-door entry
- 6'-0" x 4'-0" garden shed attached to existing structure
- Shed roof
- 4 x 4 pressure-treated runners for base—no foundation

Shed with Porch

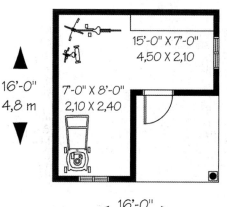

16'-0"
4,8 m

15'-0" X 7'-0"
4,50 X 2,10

7'-0" X 8'-0"
2,10 X 2,40

16'-0"
4,8 m

Plan #181134

Dimensions: 16' W x 16' D
Levels: 1
Square Footage: 192
Foundation: Slab
Materials List Available: Yes
Price Category: BB

CAD FILE AVAILABLE

- Stucco exterior
- 16'-0" x 16'-0" garden shed
- Entry porch
- Concrete slab foundation

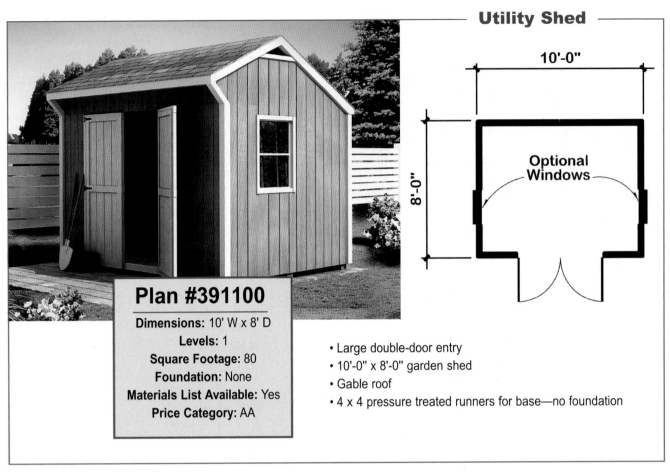

Utility Shed

10'-0"

8'-0"

Optional Windows

Plan #391100

Dimensions: 10' W x 8' D
Levels: 1
Square Footage: 80
Foundation: None
Materials List Available: Yes
Price Category: AA

- Large double-door entry
- 10'-0" x 8'-0" garden shed
- Gable roof
- 4 x 4 pressure treated runners for base—no foundation

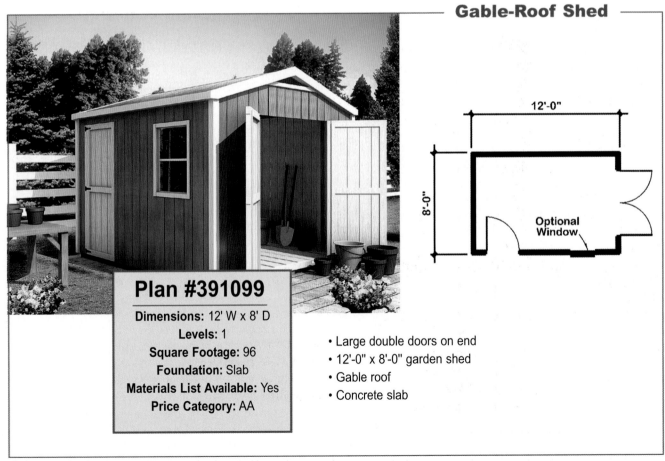

Gable-Roof Shed

12'-0"

8'-0"

Optional Window

Plan #391099

Dimensions: 12' W x 8' D
Levels: 1
Square Footage: 96
Foundation: Slab
Materials List Available: Yes
Price Category: AA

- Large double doors on end
- 12'-0" x 8'-0" garden shed
- Gable roof
- Concrete slab

Backyard Playground

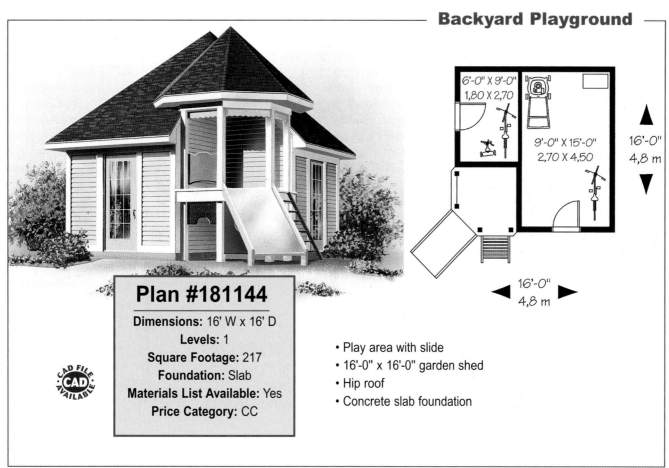

Plan #181144

Dimensions: 16' W x 16' D
Levels: 1
Square Footage: 217
Foundation: Slab
Materials List Available: Yes
Price Category: CC

CAD FILE AVAILABLE

- Play area with slide
- 16'-0" x 16'-0" garden shed
- Hip roof
- Concrete slab foundation

Gambrel Shed

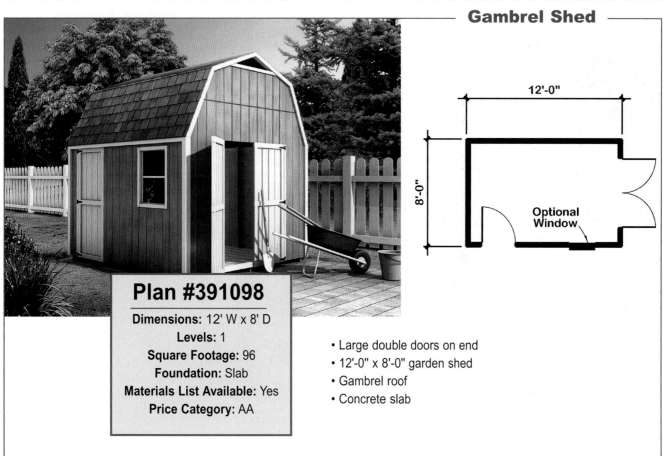

Plan #391098

Dimensions: 12' W x 8' D
Levels: 1
Square Footage: 96
Foundation: Slab
Materials List Available: Yes
Price Category: AA

- Large double doors on end
- 12'-0" x 8'-0" garden shed
- Gambrel roof
- Concrete slab

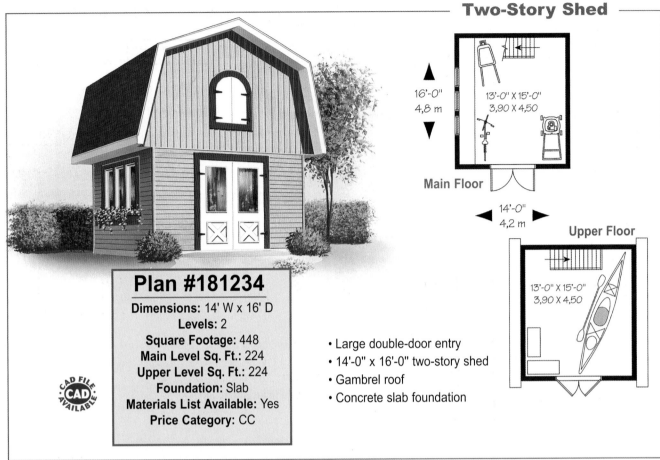

Two-Story Shed

Main Floor

16'-0"
4,8 m

13'-0" X 15'-0"
3,90 X 4,50

14'-0"
4,2 m

Upper Floor

13'-0" X 15'-0"
3,90 X 4,50

Plan #181234

Dimensions: 14' W x 16' D
Levels: 2
Square Footage: 448
Main Level Sq. Ft.: 224
Upper Level Sq. Ft.: 224
Foundation: Slab
Materials List Available: Yes
Price Category: CC

CAD FILE AVAILABLE

• Large double-door entry
• 14'-0" x 16'-0" two-story shed
• Gambrel roof
• Concrete slab foundation

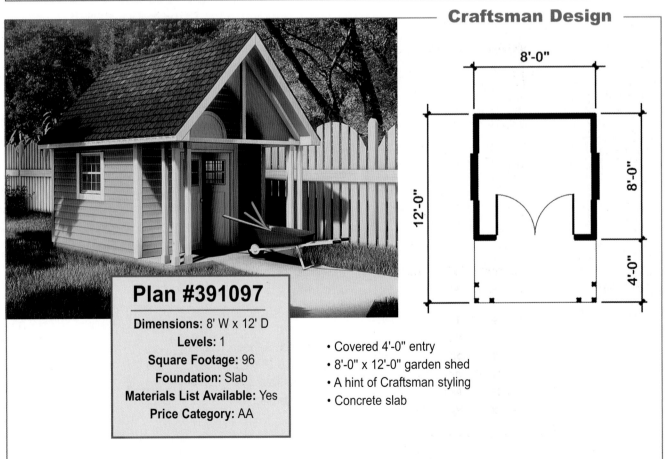

Craftsman Design

8'-0"

12'-0"

8'-0"

4'-0"

Plan #391097

Dimensions: 8' W x 12' D
Levels: 1
Square Footage: 96
Foundation: Slab
Materials List Available: Yes
Price Category: AA

• Covered 4'-0" entry
• 8'-0" x 12'-0" garden shed
• A hint of Craftsman styling
• Concrete slab

Garage Plus Storage

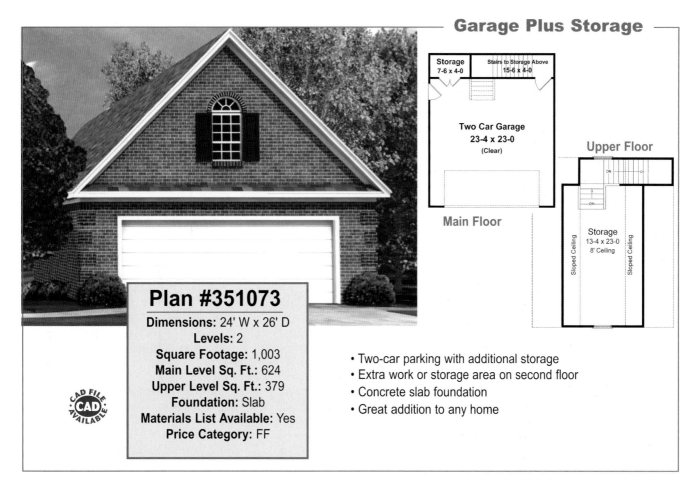

Storage
7-6 x 4-0

Stairs to Storage Above
15-6 x 4-0

Two Car Garage
23-4 x 23-0
(Clear)

Main Floor

Upper Floor

DN

DN

Storage
13-4 x 23-0
8' Ceiling

Sloped Ceiling

Sloped Ceiling

Plan #351073

Dimensions: 24' W x 26' D
Levels: 2
Square Footage: 1,003
Main Level Sq. Ft.: 624
Upper Level Sq. Ft.: 379
Foundation: Slab
Materials List Available: Yes
Price Category: FF

CAD FILE AVAILABLE

• Two-car parking with additional storage
• Extra work or storage area on second floor
• Concrete slab foundation
• Great addition to any home

Potting Shed

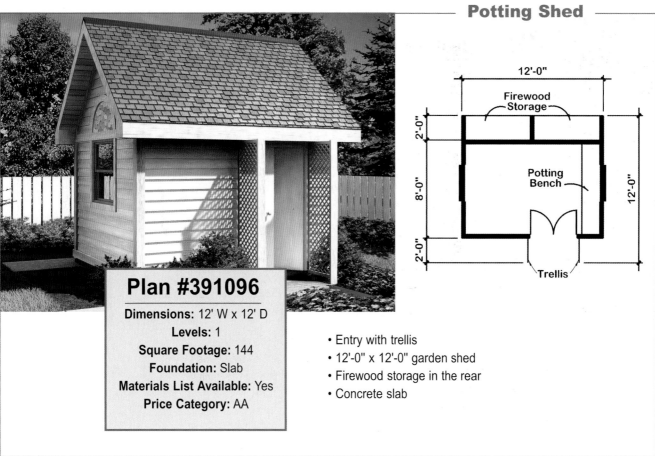

12'-0"

Firewood
Storage

2'-0"

8'-0"

2'-0"

Potting
Bench

12'-0"

Trellis

Plan #391096

Dimensions: 12' W x 12' D
Levels: 1
Square Footage: 144
Foundation: Slab
Materials List Available: Yes
Price Category: AA

• Entry with trellis
• 12'-0" x 12'-0" garden shed
• Firewood storage in the rear
• Concrete slab

Glossary

Actual dimensions The exact measurements of a piece of lumber, pipe, or masonry. See "Nominal dimensions."

Anchor bolt A bolt set in concrete that is used to fasten lumber, brackets, or hangers to concrete or masonry walls.

Apron Architectural trim beneath a window stool or sill.

Backfill Soil or gravel used to fill in between a foundation or retaining wall and the ground excavated around it.

Barge rafters The last outside rafters of a structure. They are usually nailed to outriggers and form the gable-end overhangs. Sometimes called fly rafters.

Battens Narrow wood strips that cover vertical joints between siding boards.

Beam A steel or wood framing member installed horizontally to support part of a structure's load.

Bent A complete cross-section frame assembly (typically including wall, ceiling, and roof components) in a timber-frame building.

Bird's mouth The notch made of a level and plumb cut near the tail end of a rafter where the rafter edge rests on a top plate or horizontal framing member.

Blocking Lumber added between studs, joists, rafters, or other framing members to provide a nailing surface, additional strength, spacing between boards, or firestopping.

Center pole In pole framing, the center ascending poles or posts that provide structural support for the roof and internal framing.

Chord The wood members of a truss that form the two sides of the roof and the base, or ceiling joist.

Cleat A small board fastened to a surface to provide support for another board, or any board nailed onto another board to strengthen or support it.

Collar tie A horizontal board installed rafter-to-rafter for extra support.

Corner boards Boards nailed vertically to the corners of a building that serve as a stopping point for siding and as an architectural feature.

Cupola Small ventilating structures built on top of the roof with louvered sides to allow for airflow.

Cripple studs Short studs that stand vertically between a header and top plate or between a bottom plate and the underside of a rough sill.

Curing The hardening process of concrete during which moisture is added or trapped under plastic or other sealer. Proper curing reduces cracking and shrinkage and develops strength.

Dead load The weight of a building's components, including lumber, roofing, and permanent fixtures.

Double top plate The double tier of two-by lumber running horizontally on top of and nailed to wall studs.

Drip cap Molding at the top of a window or door.

Drip edge A metal piece bent to fit over the edge of roof sheathing, designed to shed rain.

Easement The legal right for one person to cross or use another person's land. The most common easements are narrow tracts for utility lines.

Eaves The lower part of a roof that projects beyond the supporting walls to create an overhang.

Face-nailing Nailing perpendicularly through the surface of lumber.

Fascia One-by or two-by trim pieces nailed onto the end grain or tail end of a rafter to form part of a cornice or overhang.

Flashing Thin sheets of aluminum, copper, rubber asphalt, or other material used to bridge or cover a joint between materials that is exposed to the weather—for example, between the roof and a chimney.

Floor joists The long wooden beams generally set horizontally 16 inches on center between foundation walls or girders.

Footing The part of a foundation that transmits loads to the soil; also, the base on which a stone wall is built. Typical footings are twice as wide as the wall they support and at least as deep as the wall is wide.

Frost heave Shifting or upheaval of the ground resulting from alternate freezing and thawing of the moisture in soil.

Frost line The maximum depth to which soil freezes in the winter.

Full stud Vertical two-by lumber that extends from the bottom plate to the top plate of a wall.

Gable roof A roof in the shape of an inverted V with two triangular ends.

Gable end The triangular wall section under each end of a gable roof.

Gambrel roof A roof design common on barns and utility buildings that combines two gable roofs of differing slopes. The lower slope on each side is steep, which provides more usable space in lofts.

Grade The identification class of lumber quality. Also shorthand for ground level—the finished level of the ground on a building site.

Ground-fault circuit interrupter (GFCI) A device that detects a ground fault or electrical line leakage and immediately shuts down power to that circuit.

Gusset plates Metal or plywood plates used to hold together the chords and webs of a truss.

Header The thick horizontal member that runs above rough openings, such as doors and windows, in a building's frame.

Header joist A horizontal board, installed on edge, that is secured to the ends of the floor joists.

Jack rafters Short rafters, typically in a hip roof, that run at an angle between a rafter and a top plate.

Jack stud A stud that runs from the bottom plate to the underside of a header. Also called a trimmer.

Jamb The upright surface forming the side in an opening, as for a door or window.

Joist Horizontal framing lumber placed on edge to support subfloors or hold up ceilings.

Joist hanger Bracket used to strengthen the connection between a joist and a piece of lumber into which it butts.

Kerf The narrow slot a saw blade cuts in a piece of lumber, usually about $\frac{1}{8}$ inch thick.

Live load All the loads in and on a building that are not a permanent part of the structure—such as furniture, people, and wind.

Miter A joint in which two boards are joined at angles (usually 45 degrees) to form a corner.

Nailing flange An extension attached to a building component, usually predrilled for nails or screws—for example, around the sides of a window and on the edges of beam hanging hardware.

Nominal dimensions In lumber, the premilling measurement for which a piece of lumber is named (i.e., 2x4); in masonry, the measured dimensions of a masonry unit plus one mortar joint.

O.C. An abbreviation for on center, typically referring to layout measurements taken from the center of one stud to the center of the next stud.

Oriented-strand board (OSB) Panel material made of wood strands purposely aligned for strength and bonded together with adhesive.

Outrigger A projecting framing member run out from a main structure to provide additional stability or nailing for another framing component.

Overhang Typically, the extension of a roof beyond the perimeter walls; also any projection, such as a deck platform that extends beyond it's supporting girder.

Penny (Abbreviation: d.) Unit of measure for nail length, such as a 10d nail, which is 3 inches long.

Pilot hole A hole drilled before a screw is inserted to defeat splitting.

Pitch Loosely, the slope or angle of a roof; technically, the rise of a roof over its span.

Platform framing The framing method in which walls are built one story at a time on top of decked platforms over the story below.

Plumb Vertically straight. A line 90 degrees to a level line.

Prehung door A door that's already set in a jamb, with hinges (and sometimes a lockset) preassembled, ready to be installed in a rough opening.

Pressure treated Wood that has preservatives forced into it under pressure.

Purlin Roof timbers spanning between principal rafters, typically set on edge to derive maximum strength in the unsupported span.

Quality mark An ink stamp or end tag label that is applied to pressure-treated lumber (and some other lumber). The quality mark provides important information, including the type of preservative used and the water retention level.

Rake trim Trim boards applied to the fascia along the gable ends of a roof projection.

Rafter Any of the parallel framing members that support a roof.

Rebar Short for reinforcement bar, or metal bars laid in a grid used to reinforce concrete.

Ridge The horizontal crest of a roof.

Ridgeboard The horizontal board that defines the roof frame's highest point, or ridge.

Ridge cut The cut at the uphill end of a rafter, along the ridge plumb line, that allows the rafter's end grain to sit flush against the ridgeboard.

Rim joists Joists that define the outside edges of a platform. Joists that run perpendicular to floor joists and are end-nailed to joist ends are also known as header joists.

Rise In a roof, the vertical distance between the supporting wall's cap plate and the point where a line, drawn through the outside edge of the cap plate and parallel to the roof's slope, intersects the centerline of the ridgeboard.

Riser In plumbing, a water-supply pipe that carries water vertically; in carpentry, the vertical part of a stair installed on edge, across the front of the step.

Run In a roof with a ridge, the horizotal distance between the edge of an outside wall's cap plate and the centerline of the ridgeboard.

Scarf joint Where the end grain of two pieces of lumber meet in the same plane at a 45-degree angle, or in a jagged, overlapped cut, typically backed up by another board or hardware to secure the joint.

Setback A local building code that requires structures to be built a certain distance from the street, sidewalk, or property line.

Shakes Similar to cedar shingles, but rougher in texture because they are split rather than sawn.

Sheathing Panel material, typically plywood, applied to the outside of a structure. Siding is installed over it.

Shed roof A roof that slopes in one direction.

Sill The horizontal two-by lumber attached directly to the masonry foundation. It supports the building's walls. Also, the piece of wood at the bottom of a window frame, typically angled to shed water.

Skirt boards Trim that is installed along the bottom edge of the wall.

Slope The rise of a roof over its run, expressed as the number of inches of rise per unit of run (usually 12 inches). For example: 6-in-12 means a roof rises 6 inches for every 12 inches of run.

Soffit The boards or plywood panels that run the length of a wall on the underside of the rafters, covering the space between the wall and the fascia.

Soleplate The horizontal two-by lumber that forms the base of framed walls, also called a shoe.

Span Distance between supports, such as the outside walls of a building or a structural wall and a beam.

Stool A narrow shelf that butts against a windowsill.

Toenailing Driving a nail at an angle into the face of a board so that it penetrates another board beneath or above it.

Top plate The horizontal two-by board nailed to the top of wall studs, almost always consisting of two boards that overlap at corners.

Total rise The ridge height of a roof measured from the top plate of the structure's wall.

Total run One half the building span, used in the calculation of roof angles.

Trim Typically one-by lumber used as siding corner boards or as finish materials around windows and doors, under eaves, or with other architectural elements.

Trimmer Another term for a jack stud, or the short stud (nailed onto a full stud) that supports a header.

Truss A rigid assembly of timbers relying on triangulation to span distances impractical for a single member.

Valley flashing Material used to prevent leaks at the intersection of two pitched roofs that form an internal angle.

Web The inner members of a truss that carry loads from the chords, or perimeter members.

Wind load The stress on a structure due to gusting winds.

Z-brace door Door construction typically consisting of boards joined together and strengthened by a series of braces screwed to the backs of the boards in a Z-shaped pattern.

Resources

The following list of manufacturers and associations is meant to be a general guide to additional industry and product-related sources. It is not intended as a listing of products and manufacturers represented by the photographs in this book.

APA—THE ENGINEERED WOOD ASSOCIATION

P.O. Box 11700
Tacoma, WA 98411
www.apawood.org
APA is a nonprofit trade association, the U.S. and Canadian members of which produce a variety of engineered wood products. Primary functions include quality inspection and product promotion. Write for free brochures.

THE FLOOD COMPANY

800-321-3444
www.floodco.com
Flood is a 150-year-old family-owned corporation that makes a variety of paint-related products, including penetrating stains, sealers, wood renewers, and cleaners. The company Web site offers a full rundown of products, information on application tools, and a store locator.

HANDY HOME PRODUCTS

6400 E. 11 Mile Rd.
Warren, MI 48091
800-221-1849
www.handyhome.com
Handy Home Products is a leader in ready-to-assemble wooden storage buildings, gazebos, timber buildings, and children's playhouses. Call or write with inquiries.

INTERNATIONAL CODE COUNCIL (ICC)

5203 Leesburg Pike, Ste. 600
Falls Church, VA 22041
703-931-4533
www.iccsafe.org
The International Code Council provides the construction codes and standards that are used on job sites throughout the country. By combining the efforts of various regional code organizations, ICC has created a universal set of requirements for construction in the United States.

LOUISIANA-PACIFIC CORPORATION

805 S.W. Broadway
Portland, OR 97205
800-648-6893
www.lpcorp.com
LP is a premier supplier of commodity and specialty building products serving the retail, wholesale, homebuilding, and industrial markets. Visit the Web site for questions or information.

NORTH AMERICAN INSULATION MANUFACTURERS ASSOCIATION (NAIMA)

44 Canal Center Plaza #310
Alexandria, VA 22312
703-684-0084
www.naima.org
NAIMA is a trade association of manufacturers of fiberglass, rock wool, and slag wool insulation products. Visit its Web site for publications on these products.

PORTER-CABLE CORPORATION

4825 Hwy. 45 North, P.O. Box 2468
Jackson, TN 38302
800-487-8665
www.porter-cable.com
Porter-Cable is a leading manufacturer of portable electric and cordless power tools, nailers, compressors, and related accessories for commercial and residential construction, plumbing, and electrical markets.

RYOBI NORTH AMERICA

1424 Pearman Dairy Rd.
Anderson, SC 29625
800-525-2579
www.ryobi.com
Ryobi produces portable and bench-top power tools for contractors and DIYers. It also manufactures a line of lawn and garden tools. Call its toll-free customer service line for free literature, or go on-line.

SIMPSON STRONG-TIE COMPANY

4637 Chabot Dr., Ste. 200
Pleasanton, CA 94588
800-999-5099
www.strongtie.com
One of the most widely used brands of framing hardware, with hundreds of different fasteners. Call for a free catalog or for plans for a variety of home projects.

SOUTHERN PINE COUNCIL

P.O. Box 641700
Kenner, LA 70064
www.southernpine.com
A nonprofit trade promotion group supported by manufacturers of Southern Pine lumber. For construction details and building tips, complete project plans, and other helpful information, write for a free catalog.

SPIRIT ELEMENTS

6672 Gunpark Dr, Ste. 200
Boulder, CO 80301
800-511-1440
www.spiritelements.com
Spirit Elements manufacturers shed kits, log cabins, gazebos, and other outdoor and garden structures.

THE STANLEY WORKS

1000 Stanley Dr.
New Britain, CT 06053
800-782-6539
www.stanleyworks.com
The Stanley Works provides a line of hand and power tools for contractors and homeowners. Its speciality products include a series of ergonomically designed products and a line of extra-durable contractor tools for the job site.

SUMMERWOOD PRODUCTS

733 Progress Ave.
Toronto, Ontario M1H 2W7
800-663-5042
www.summerwood.com
Summerwood Products offers dozens of shed and gazebo designs, each with many configuration options and extras. The company also sells its products in precut kits that can easily be assembled in a weekend.

WERNER CO.

93 Werner Rd.
Greenville, PA 16125
724-588-8600
www.wernerladder.com
Supplies aluminum, wood, and fiberglass ladders, step stools, and ladder accessories, such as planks and platforms. See the company's Web site for a photo gallery of its products in action.

WOLMANIZED WOOD

Arch Wood Protection, Inc.
1955 Lake Park Drive, Ste. 100
Smyrna, GA 30080
866-789-4567
www.wolmanizedwood.com
Manufactures various forms of treated lumber for diverse projects. Read more about its offerings at the company's Web site.

Index

Photo Credits

Page 1: Simon McBride/Redcover.com **page 2:** Donna Chiarelli/CH **page 6:** *both* Eric Roth **page 8:** Tria Giovan **page 10:** *top* Jessie Walker; *bottom* Andrew Kline/CH **page 11:** *top & center* Andrew Kline/CH; *bottom* Jerry Pavia **pages 12–13:** Tony Giammarino/Giammarino & Dworkin **pages 14–15:** Jerry Pavia **page 17:** *top* Ed Reeve/Redcover.com; *bottom* Tony Giammarino/Giammarino & Dworkin **page 18:** *top* James Mejuto; *bottom* Jerry Pavia **page 19:** Jessie Walker **page 20:** Eric Roth **page 21:** Tony Giammarino/Giammarino & Dworkin **page 22:** Simon McBride/Redcover.com **page 23:** *top* Tony Giammarino/Giammarino & Dworkin; *bottom* Hugh Palmer/Redcover.com **page 24:** Eric Roth **page 26:** Jessie Walker **page 27:** *top right, center right* Tony Giammarino/Giammarino & Dworkin; *bottom* Jessie Walker; *top left* Chris Brink/Redcover.com **page 28:** Eric Roth **page 29:** *top* Bradley Olman **page 31:** *top* Tria Giovan; *bottom* Jessie Walker **page 32:** Hugh Palmer/Redcover.com **page 33:** *top* Eric Roth; *bottom* Tony Giammarino/Giammarino & Dworkin **pages 34–35:** John Parsekian/CH **page 36:** Brian C. Nieves/CH **page 37:** *top both* John Parsekian/CH; *left center, bottom left* Brian C. Nieves/CH; *bottom right* courtesy of Paslode **page 38:** *top both* Brian C. Nieves/CH; *bottom both* John Parsekian/CH **page 39:** *both* John Parsekian/CH **page 40:** *top* Brian C. Nieves/CH; *bottom both* John Parsekian/CH **page 41:** *both* John Parsekian/CH **page 45:** Brian C. Nieves/CH **page 46:** John Parsekian/CH **page 47:** *all* John Parsekian/CH **page 48:** *top right* courtesy of Louisiana Pacific; *bottom both, top left* courtesy of APA, The Engineered Wood Association **page 49:** courtesy of APA, The Engineered Wood Association **pages 52–53:** Donna Chiarelli/CH **page 55:** *all* John Parsekian/CH **page 56:** *top* John Parsekian/CH; *bottom both* Brian C. Nieves/CH **page 57:** *top* John Puleio; *bottom both* Brian C. Nieves/CH **page 58:** *all* John Parsekian/CH **pages 60–63:** *all* John Parsekian/CH **page 64:** *top left* John Parsekian/CH; *top right, center row* Brian C. Nieves **pages 66–67:** Donna Chiarelli/Ch **pages 68–70:** Brian C. Nieves/CH **page 72:** both Brian C. Nieves/CH **pages 74–75:** *all* John Parsekian/CH **page 80:** Brian C. Nieves/CH **page 81:** John Parsekian/CH **pages 84–85:** *all* Brian C. Nieves/CH **page 86:** courtesy of Better Barns **page 89:** *all* Brian C. Nieves/CH **page 90:** Brian C. Nieves/CH **page 91:** *top* Dan Lane/CH; *bottom three* Brian C. Nieves/CH **pages 92–94:** *all* Brian C. Nieves/CH **page 95:** *all* Merle Henkenius **page 96:** Andrew Kline/CH **page 97:** *top right* Donna Chiarelli/CH; *bottom right, bottom left* Andrew Kline/CH; *top left* John Puleio/CH **pages 98–99:** Donna Chiarelli/CH **pages 102–125:** Donna Chiarelli/CH **pages 126–127:** Andrew Kline/CH **pages 130–143:** John Puleio/CH **pages 144–145:** Andrew Kline/CH **pages 149–179:** John Puleio/CH **pages 180–181:** Andrew Kline/CH **pages 184–191:** John Puleio/CH **page 203:** Tony Giammarino/Giammarino & Dworkin; **page 207:** Jessie Walker; **back cover:** *top* Donna Chiarelli/CH; *bottom left, bottom right* John Puleio/CH; *bottom center* Donna Chiarelli/CH

Have a home gardening, decorating, or improvement project? Look for these and other fine Creative Homeowner books wherever books are sold.

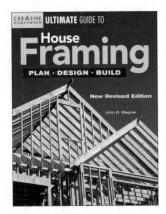

Designed to walk you through the framing basics. 750+ photos and illos. 240 pp.; 8½"×10⅞"
BOOK#: 277660

A complete guide covering all aspects of drywall. Over 325 color illustrations.160 pp.; 8½"×10⅞"
BOOK #: 278320

Guide to designing and building decks. Over 650 color photos. 288 pp.; 8½"×10⅞"
BOOK #: 277168

Everything you need to know about setting ceramic tile. Over 450 photos. 224 pp.; 8½"×10⅞"
BOOK#: 277532

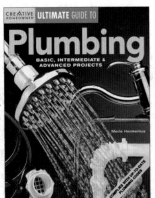

The complete manual for plumbing projects. Over 750 color photos and illustrations. 272 pp.; 8½"×10⅞"
BOOK#: 278210

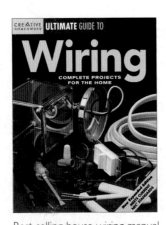

Best-selling house-wiring manual. Over 840 color photos and illustrations. 288 pp.; 8½"×10⅞"
BOOK#: 278237

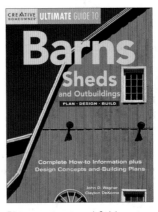

Plan, construct, and finish outbuildings. 850+ color photos and illustrations. 208 pp.; 8½"×10⅞"
BOOK#: 277812

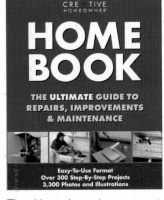

The ultimate home improvement reference manual. Over 300 step-by-step projects. 608 pp.; 9"×10⅞"
BOOK#: 267855

How to create kitchen style like a pro. Over 500 photos and illos. 224 pp.; 8½"×10⅞"
BOOK #: 279415

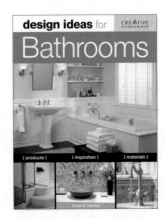

All you need to know about designing a bath. Over 475 color photos. 224 pp.; 8½"×10⅞"
BOOK #: 279268

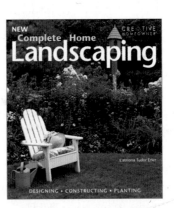

An impressive guide to landscape design and plant selection. More than 950 color photos. 384 pp.; 9"×10"
BOOK #: 274610

Lavishly illustrated with portraits of over 100 flowering plants; more than 500 photos. 208 pp.; 9"×10"
BOOK #: 274032

For more information, and to order direct, go to www.creativehomeowner.com